ו
ז
ח
ט
י
כ
ל
מ
נ
ס
ע
פ
צ
ק
ר
ש
ת

Origins of the Alphabet

Other titles in this series:

1. INTRODUCING ARCHAEOLOGY
2. ANCIENT POTTERY
3. JEWELLERY IN ANCIENT TIMES
4. ANCIENT SCROLLS
5. ANCIENT MOSAICS
7. UNDERWATER ARCHAEOLOGY
8. WEAPONS OF THE ANCIENT WORLD
9. INTRODUCING PREHISTORY

Cassell's Introducing Archaeology Series

Origins of the Alphabet

JOSEPH NAVEH

Cassell · London

CASSELL & COMPANY
35 Red Lion Square, London WC1R 4SG
Sydney, Auckland
Toronto, Johannesburg

Designed by Ofra Kamar

First published in Great Britain 1975

I.S.B.N. 0 304 29336 9

Printed by Peli Printing Works, Ltd., Givataim

PRINTED IN ISRAEL

F. 873

CONTENTS

FOREWORD

This book describes the development of the alphabet in ancient times. The alphabet was introduced by the Semites; in fact it was primarily a Semitic method of writing. The Canaanites developed the first alphabet in the middle of the 2nd millennium BC; gradually, other Semitic peoples and the ancient Greeks learned this way of writing. Each nation developed its own independent script, basing itself on the Canaanite prototype.

Some of these nations — the Phoenicians, the Aramaeans, and the Nabataeans — no longer exist today. But their contribution to surviving alphabets was very important. Other nations, like the Jews and the Greeks, have survived, preserving their ancient writing traditions until modern times. The Latin and Cyrillic scripts both developed from the Greek alphabet: the Latin script is the most common alphabet in use today, while Cyrillic writing is used mainly in the U.S.S.R., Bulgaria and Yugoslavia.

The story is divided into two sections. In the first one, I shall try to explain the relationships between the various scripts, and their historical background. I shall also follow their development, for scripts grow like a tree which puts forth several branches. In the second section I shall trace the individual developments of each letter. In the earliest stages of writing, letters were drawn like pictures. There were many changes over the years in the various scripts, and I shall follow these changes up to the crystallization of the modern letter forms in the Jewish (square Hebrew), Arabic, Greek, and Latin alphabets.

SECTION ONE

Introduction

Language distinguishes man from animal, but the knowledge of writing is the hallmark of *civilized* man. Language and writing are ways of cultural expression. They reflect both individual and collective cultures. One of the greatest achievements in man's history is his development of graphic signs for the systematic recording of the spoken language. Inscribed artefacts from archaeological excavations show that man had a knowledge of writing as early as the late 4th millennium BC. Writing marks the beginning of the historical era. In the pre-historic and proto-historic periods, people could not write: wall drawings and pictures on rocks expressed the thoughts and wishes of these primitive men. But the earliest inscriptions from the historical era use a series of pictures to express single words.

Sumerian pictographic script

The inscriptions have been found at various sites on the banks of the great rivers of the Near East. In Mesopotamia, the Sumerians introduced a pictographic script in the late 4th millennium BC.

Fragment of a clay tablet with cuneiform script

This picture-writing gradually developed into the cuneiform or wedge-shaped script. Cuneiform writing was produced by marking soft clay with a pointed object (stylus). It had many signs for syllables and words. Many ancient peoples later adopted cuneiform writing, including the Eastern Semites, namely the Akkadians, Babylonians, and Assyrians, and non-Semites such as the Hurrians, Elamites, and Hittites.

The ancient Egyptians developed another pictographic script. The Greeks named it "hieroglyphs", meaning "engraving of holy texts", but the Egyptians also wrote secular texts in this script. Sometimes it was engraved into hard objects, sometimes written on soft materials such as papyrus. The hieroglyphic script consisted of word-pic-

Cuneiform writing on an Old-Babylonian cylinder seal (below) and its impression (above)

tures, syllable-pictures, and letter-pictures. It used only consonants and did not determine vowels.

Pictographic scripts were also born in Anatolia and in Crete. In Anatolia, the Hittites developed pictographs, although they also used Sumerian cuneiform. From Cretan pictographs, the Linear B script of Mycenaean Greece was developed, a syllabic writing which has only recently been deciphered.

In the 2nd millennium BC, four writing systems existed in the four corners of the ancient world. The Hittites in the north used the Hittite pictographic script, while the Egyptians

Egyptian hieroglyphic writing

Egyptian writing on papyrus

Cretan pictographic inscription

Hittite pictographic inscription carved in relief

in the south wrote with hieroglyphs. In the west, the Minoan–Mycenaean script was written. Sumerian cuneiform was used in the east. The number of signs in all these scripts was very large. The knowledge of writing was, therefore, limited to narrow circles of people.

Eventually, the number of signs was reduced. This marks the introduction of the alphabet. It began in the central area of the ancient world, in the middle of the Fertile Crescent. The beginnings of the modern alphabet stem from the land where various cultures met—the land of Canaan.

The universally employed alphabetic method of writing is so simple that most of us take it for granted and do not fully appreciate an invention dating from some 3,600 years ago. However, even in our modern times, certain peoples still use complicated systems of writing. The Chinese and the Japanese, for example, use many hundreds and even thousands of symbols for expressing their language in writing. In 1946, in Japan, an attempt was made to reduce the number of writing symbols to 1850, of which 881 were to be taught in elementary schools. These numbers sound incredible to the Western mind, since English-speaking peoples are able to represent their language in 26 letters.

Linear B script

The introduction of the alphabet by Western Semites in ancient times can be evaluated only by bearing in mind that the surrounding peoples (Egyptians, Hittites and Babylonians) used scripts almost as complicated as those of the Chinese and the Japanese. Western Semites brought the alphabet to Greece, whence it spread to all the countries of the Western world. The invention of the alphabet meant that everyone could learn to read and write with ease. This great innovation enabled even the poorest peasant to read, where before only priests and persons of high standing could benefit from the written word.

1. *The Rise of the Alphabet*

Man has always been curious to know how alphabetic script began. Herodotus, the "father of history", mentions that the Phoenicians came to Greece with a man named Kadmos. There they introduced writing and other arts. This idea was commonly accepted by Greek and Roman writers. Some of them developed it even further. Plato and Tacitus state that the Phoenicians learned the art of writing from the Egyptians. Diodorus Siculus and Pliny claim that the Phoenicians learnt from the Assyrians. In the 19th century, some scholars believed these theories; others believed that the Phoenician script developed from the Cypro-Minoan writing or even from the Hittite pictographic script.

In 1905, Sir Flinders Petrie discovered some inscriptions of a peculiar kind at Serabit el-Khadem in the Sinai Peninsula. They were called Proto-Sinaitic inscriptions. Interest in these writings started modern investigation into the origin of the alphabet. Petrie's texts contained about 25 to 30 pictographic signs. These were inscribed approximately in the middle of the 2nd millennium BC. In 1916, Sir Alan Gardiner took the first steps toward the decipherment of these texts. He noted a recurrent series of pictographs – oxgoad-house-eye-oxgoad-cross and recognized that the signs followed an acrophonic principle. This means that each picture presents the first consonant of a Canaanite word beginning with this letter. The signs for the pictures *lamed-bet-ʻayin-lamed-taw* should equal the Canaanite word *"lbʻlt" (le-baʻalat)*. This means "for the Lady" and is a favourite name for the Canaanite goddess Ashera.

Since then, many attempts at decipherment of this script have been made. The best known is that of W.F. Albright. He believed that it was possible to identify twenty-three out of the probable twenty-seven letters occurring in these texts. Albright accepted Gardiner's acrophonic theory. He assumed

Right: Proto-Sinaitic inscription from Serabit el-Khadem. The letters at the bottom comprise the word *lbʻlt*

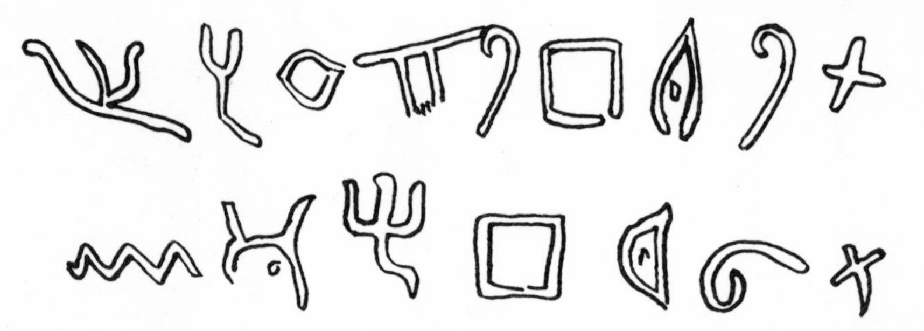

Above: A Proto-Sinaitic inscription. Last letters at the top: *lb'lt;* at the bottom: *m' hb 'lt*—"Swear to give a sacrifice" (Albright). *Below:* An early Proto-Canaanite text from Gezer: *klb,* presumably the biblical name "Caleb"

that these texts were votive inscriptions (dedicated to the deities) written by West Semites who worked for the Egyptians in the turquoise mines of Serabit el-Khadem. Albright's readings were based on recent knowledge of the Canaanite dialects (mainly Ugaritic) from the 2nd millennium BC.

For several decades it was assumed that these West Semite workers (or slaves) invented the first alphabetic writing because they were in daily contact with the Egyptian hieroglyphs. But several similar pictographic inscriptions were found at some sites in Palestine. Most of these—from Lachish, Tell el-Hesi, Beth Shemesh, and other places—are of a later date than the Proto-Sinaitic texts (the texts from Sinai). But at least three—from Shechem, Gezer, and Lachish—are earlier than the Proto-Sinaitic inscriptions. The collection of early Palestinian inscriptions consists of inscribed sherds and jars. But there are also inscriptions on seals, a dagger and javelin heads. The latest specimens date from the end of the Late Bronze period and from the very beginning of the Iron Age. These display simplified linear letter forms which developed from the early pictographs. The script of these is called Proto-Canaanite.

The Proto-Canaanite alphabet seems to copy some pictographic signs from the Egyptian hieroglyphs. But the in-

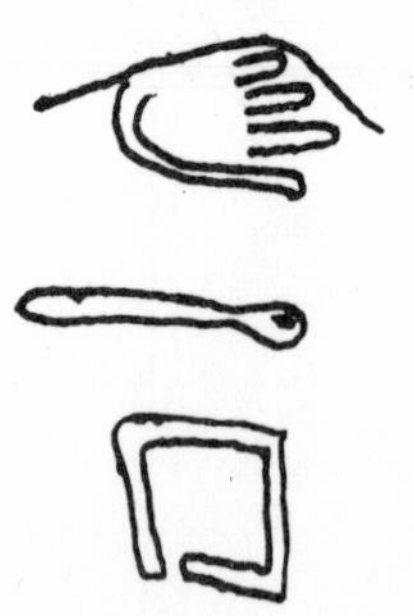

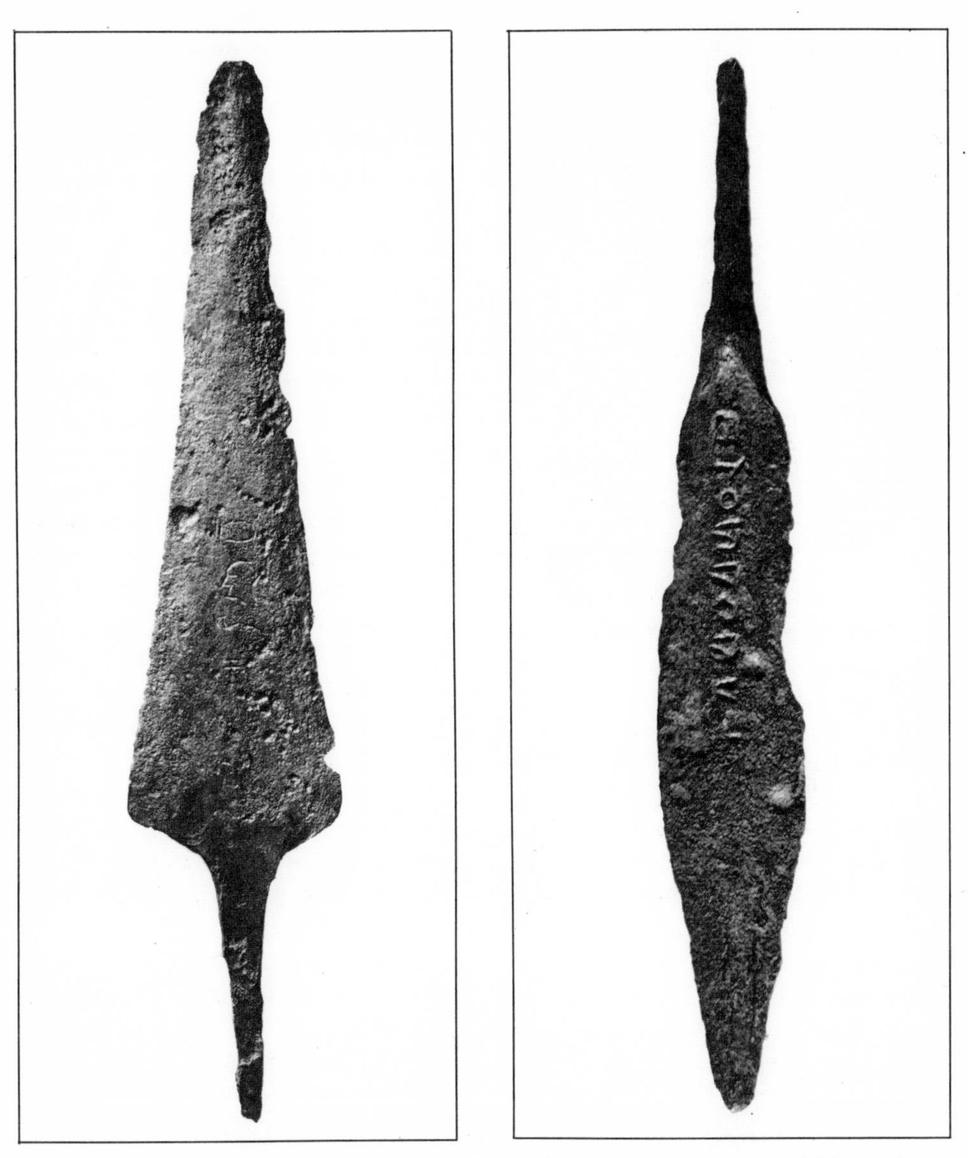

An early Proto-Canaanite inscription on a dagger found at Lachish

Javelin head found near Bethlehem with a twelfth-century BC Proto-Canaanite inscription

A fragment of a cuneiform alphabetic text from Ugarit

habitants of Ugarit in northern Canaan and other Canaanite communities adapted the writing techniques used for the Akkadian cuneiform syllabic script (clay tablet and stylus) to the new alphabetic system. (Akkadian was an international means of communication in the later half of the 2nd millennium. It was even used for correspondence between the Egyptian Pharaoh and his vassals in Palestine.) But the cuneiform alphabet was not limited to Ugarit, where rich archives of this type of script have been found. Specimens also appeared at three sites in Palestine — Beth Shemesh, Ta'anach, and near Mount Tabor. But as far as we know, the cuneiform alphabet ceased to be used with the beginning of the Iron Age in the 12th century BC. The Proto-Canaanite script, on the other hand, was the source of all alphabetic scripts which later spread throughout the entire world.

The following order of the early alphabetic scripts is suggested by F.M. Cross, Jr.:

I. The Proto-Canaanite Texts
   a) Old Palestinian (17th–12th centuries BC)
   b) Proto-Sinaitic (15th century BC)

II. Canaanite Cuneiform Texts
   a) Ugaritic (14th–13th centuries BC)
   b) Palestinian (13th–12th centuries BC).

During the 14th and 13th centuries BC, Proto-Arabic script branched off from the Proto-Canaanite script. (Proto-Arabic is the parent script of South Arabic monumental writing and the Ethiopic script, as well as the Thamudic, Safaitic, and Lihyanic scripts.) But the main offshoots of the Proto-Canaanite script are the Phoenician and the Greek alphabets. From Phoenician evolved (ancient) Hebrew and Aramaic. All European scripts came from the Greek alphabet.

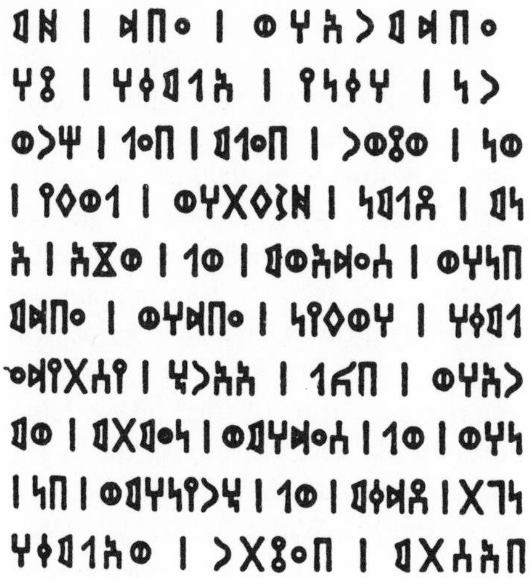

South Arabian monumental inscription

2. *The Term "Alphabetic Script"*

It has been said that the term *alphabetic* does not fit West Semitic writing (Phoenician, Hebrew, Aramaic, and their derivatives). In I. J. Gelb's opinion, these scripts are systems of syllabic writing. He argued that because each sign represents a consonant plus any vowel (or zero vowel) it cannot be regarded as a purely alphabetic script. It is true that the West Semitic system of writing is less developed than the Greek, which also uses vowel letters. But the term *alphabet* does not mean that each letter must stand for either a consonant or a vowel, or for a consonant plus any vowel. *Alphabet* means a limited number of letters (twenty to thirty) listed in a fixed order. The individual value of each letter is not important to the definition.

The first list of letters in alphabetical order (a so-called abecedary) known till now was found in Ugarit. It belongs to the 14th century BC. Its order, after omitting some letters, generally fits that of the Hebrew and Greek alphabets. In the West Semitic writing the symbols were reduced to represent units of consonants. This made it easier for people to learn to read, and was the most significant development

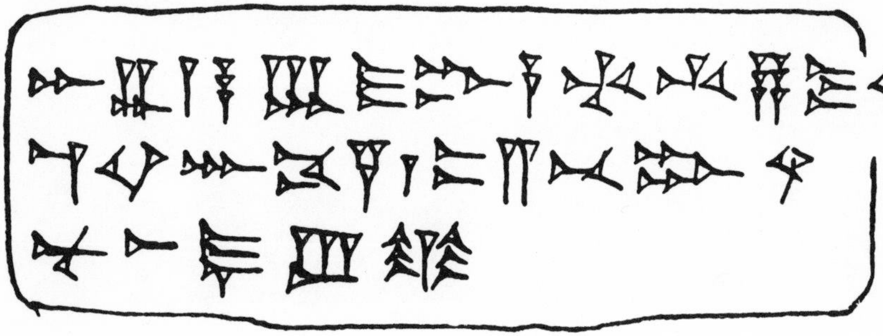

Ugaritic abecedary

towards spreading literacy. The systematic insertion of vowel signs into the script was a further step in this process. There is no reason, therefore, to restrict the term *alphabet* to Greek or Latin scripts and to their descendants.

3. *The Phoenician Script*

The Proto-Canaanite and the cuneiform alphabetic scripts (as well as the South Arabic) have 27 to 30 letters. The cuneiform alphabet distinguishes between *'alef*-a, *'alef*-i, and *'alef*-u. The Proto-Canaanite inscriptions were written either in vertical columns, or in horizontal lines, or in *boustrophedon*. (*Boustrophedon* is a technical term which means script that is written from right to left and from left to right in alternate lines; the word compares this sort of writing to ploughing oxen, which walk across a field from left to right and return from right to left.) Approximately in the 13th century, the number of letters in Proto-Canaanite script was reduced to 22. Then in the 11th century, the development of the linear letter forms had been accomplished. At the same time the right-to-left direction was stabilized. With these developments, the name of the script changes from Proto-Canaanite to Phoenician. The inscription found at Byblos on the

The Ahiram sarcophagus

Part of the inscription on the Ahiram sarcophagus

Ahiram sarcophagus (which dates to about 1000 BC) displays the end product of this evolution. The Phoenician phonemic system (the set of single speech sounds used in a language) consisted of 22 consonants. The Hebrew and Aramaic phonemic systems, however, were richer than the Phoenician. When the Hebrews and Aramaeans adopted the Phoenician script, they could not express in

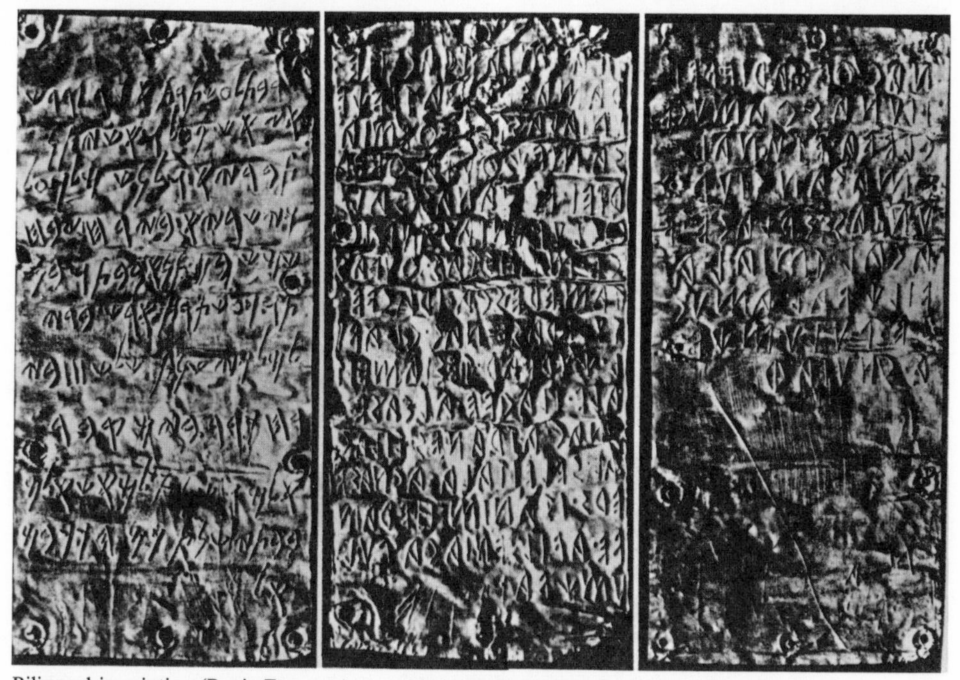

Bilingual inscription (Punic-Etruscan) on gold sheets found at Pyrgi, Italy. 5th century BC

writing certain sounds which did not occur in the Phoenician language. In Hebrew, for example, the two sounds š and ś (nowadays pronounced as *sh* and *s*) are designated by the same letter — shin. Only later, when the distinguishing diacritic signs were invented, was it possible to distinguish between שׁ (šin) and שׂ (śin).

The Phoenicians were merchants who traded throughout the ancient world. Phoenician inscriptions of the 7th century BC have been found as far apart as Ur in South Mesopotamia and Spain. Most Phoenician inscriptions, however, originate in Phoenicia, Cyprus and Carthage. The inscriptions which were found in Carthage and in the other western Phoenician colonies are called Punic. Although it is possible to note differences in the spoken dialects of Phoenicia proper, Cyprus and the Punic colonies, no special characteristics developed in the scripts of the various centres. This one-way evolution is reflected in the scarce cursive (a flowing style of writing) material, as written with ink. It is, however, especially obvious in the many monumental (mainly votive) inscriptions. Phoenician inscriptions of eastern origin after the 3rd century BC are rare. But the number of Punic inscriptions (mainly from Carthage) increases in the late 3rd and early 2nd centuries until Carthage was destroyed in 146 BC. After the destruction of Carthage, the Phoenician script continued to be used in the Neo-Punic communities in North Africa until it ceased to exist in the 2nd century AD.

Punic votive inscription from Carthage

4. *The Hebrew Script*

The Hebrews adopted the alphabetic script together with other cultural values

A fragment of a 5th–4th century BC abecedary, with the letters Z Ḥ Ṭ Y K L incised on a potsherd in the cursive Phoenician script.

from the Canaanites in the 12th or 11th century BC. They followed the current Phoenician script until the 9th century, when they began to develop their own national way of writing.

The Gezer Calendar (usually dated to the time of Solomon) is considered to be the earliest Hebrew inscription known up to the present. Its writing resembles the scripts of the tenth-century Phoenician inscriptions from Byblos (Aḥiram, Yeḥimilk, Eliba'al, Shiptiba'al). Although it seems strange, the earliest clearly Hebrew characters which can be discerned appear in the ninth-century BC inscriptions of Mesha, king of Moab. The Moabites were under the political and cultural influence of Israel. They adopted the Hebrew script for writing texts in their own dialect.

Hebrew inscriptions from the 8th century BC exhibit many traits which

Left: The Gezer calendar, 10th century BC

Above: The Moabite Stone, the stele of Mesha king of Moab

are peculiar to the Hebrew script. This makes it obvious that in the 9th century, Hebrew script was written by a large circle of scribes. Up to the present, no Hebrew inscriptions have been found from the 9th century BC, but this is purely fortuitous. The quantity of writings from the 8th century BC and onwards shows that the knowledge of writing had gradually increased among the people of Israel and Judah (cf. Judges, viii, 14, where a young man of a small city is described as being able to write).

As the independent Hebrew script evolved, it developed a special cursive character. As it moved farther away from the Phoenician mother script, it dropped many of the features it had when it was mainly engraved into stone and other hard materials. This one-trend development is obvious in the eighth-century BC engraved inscriptions such as the Siloam tunnel inscription, the epitaph of the Royal Steward and other tomb-inscriptions (all found in Jerusalem). It is also obvious on more than a hundred Hebrew seals of the 8th to

The Siloam tunnel inscription

A seventh-century BC Hebrew seal and its impression

6th centuries BC from various sites, and on a fragmentary Hebrew inscription on ivory which was taken as booty to Nimrud, probably from Samaria. These inscriptions on hard material were written in a cursive style. They even copy the shading which is a natural feature of pen-and-ink writing. The lack of Hebrew lapidary script, the style of script practised for engraving on hard objects, may indicate that the kings of Israel were not accustomed to setting-up engraved stone columns and offering votive inscriptions to the gods, so that the lapidary style disappeared from the Hebrew script.

There is some indication that papyrus — an ancient reed paper — was commonly used. In addition to the seventh-century BC papyrus fragment preserved in the dry climate of the Murabba'at Cave near the Dead Sea, about 20 clay sealings of papyrus rolls were found. But the majority of Hebrew inscriptions survived as writing on pottery. The most important of these items are the so-called ostraca (inscribed sherds) of Arad and Lachish from the last years of the Judaean Monarchy before the destruction of the First Temple of Jerusalem. These ostraca reflect the most developed type of cursive Hebrew writing.

An ostracon from Arad. Early 6th century BC

When the Babylonians captured Judah, most of the nobles were taken into exile, but the Hebrew script did not cease to exist. It was used by people who remained to work on the fields. In the 6th century BC jar handles found at Gibeon were inscribed with the names of wine-growers. In the 5th and 4th centuries BC, the Aramaic language and script were in Judah the official means of communication. The Hebrew script (called also Palaeo-Hebrew — i.e., the ancient Hebrew characters as used in the time of the Second Temple) was however still used for writing Hebrew both in Judah and in Samaria. It was preserved mainly by learned scribes as a script for copying the Bible. But the Hasmonaean coins and even the coins of the First and Second Jewish Revolts (1st and 2nd centuries AD) use Palaeo-Hebrew legends. This script is unchanging and formal. It seems likely that the Hasmonaeans used it for practical reasons, and not out of a desire to revive a forgotten national script. They struck coins with legends in a well known writing which had survived — though in a narrow circle — into the period of the Second Temple.

In Wadi Daliyeh, Aramaic deeds were discovered which were written in Samaria in the 4th century BC. Along with these were two clay sealings with Hebrew texts in the Palaeo-Hebrew script, without any Samaritan peculiarities. It seems likely that the Samaritan script began to diverge from the Palaeo-Hebrew in the last two centuries of the 1st millennium BC. The Samaritans have continued to use this script for writing both Hebrew and the

Fragment of a Pentateuch Scroll from Qumran written in Palaeo-Hebrew script

Samaritan inscription, *ca.* 4th century AD

Western Aramaic dialect they spoke. The Jews, however, ceased using it after Bar-Kochba's defeat in AD 135.

5. *The Aramaic Script and Its Offshoots*

The Aramaeans adopted the Phoenician script in the 11th or 10th century BC. The first Aramaic monumental inscriptions originated in the Aramaean kingdoms (Damascus, Hamat and Sam'al) in the 9th and 8th centuries BC. These were written in the Phoenician script. The earliest clearly Aramaic features can be discerned in the cursive script of the middle of the 8th century BC. In this period, the Assyrians introduced the Aramaic script

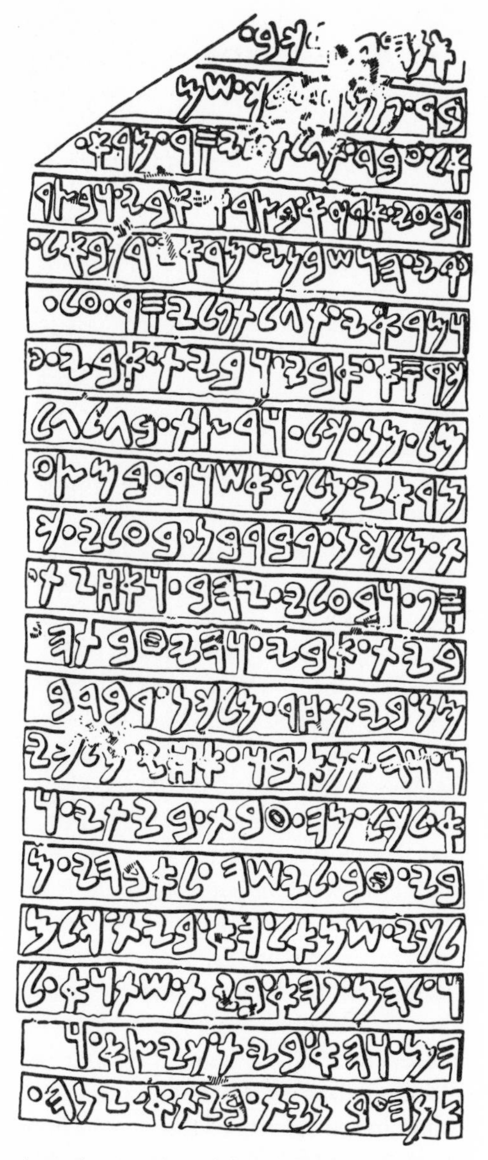

Aramaic monumental inscription of Bar-Rakib king of Sam'al – late 8th century BC

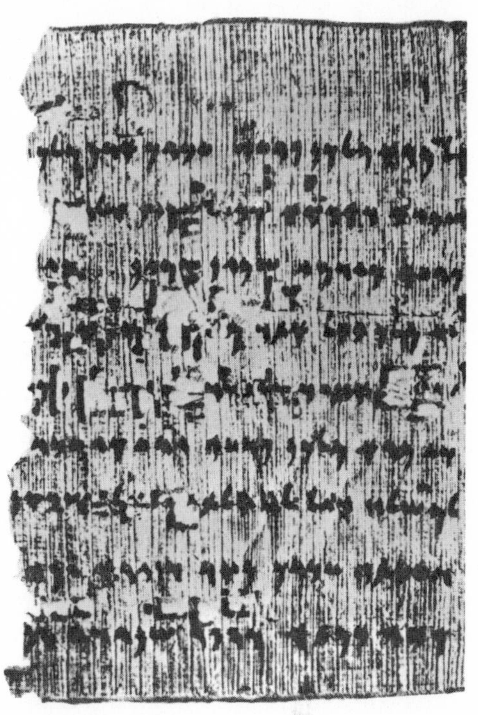

The Aramaic papyrus found at Saqqarah in Egypt, *ca.* 600 BC

and language as a common means of communication among the various nations who lived under the Assyrian rule. Finally, Aramaic became a common language, and was used from then on as an international diplomatic and commercial language. For example, an Aramaic papyrus letter sent from Palestine about 600 BC was found at Saqqarah in Egypt.

Comparative table of the Aramaic Hebrew and Phoenician cursive letters, early 6th century BC

It is most instructive to compare the Aramaic script of the Saqqarah letter, and other Aramaic cursive material of the same time, with the contemporary Phoenician and Hebrew cursive scripts (such as the inscribed fragments found at Arad and Lachish). It should be remembered that Aramaic script began to develop independently one hundred years later than Hebrew.

Aramaic script looks like shorthand in comparison with the Phoenician and, particularly, the Hebrew scripts. This is because different geographical, political, and cultural factors acted on the peoples who used these various scripts. The Phoenician script was relatively widely used by this trading people, but it remained a national script. The Hebrew script was conservative because it was developed by a nation which clung to its traditional values. After the fall of Samaria in the late 8th century BC, the Hebrew script was mostly restricted to Judah. It was written by people who dwelled in a mountainous land away from international highways. The Aramaic script, on the other hand, was used by many peoples. For this region it became a strictly practical script, with no sentiment or tradition about it.

Inscriptions found at various sites in Transjordan give a clear picture of the writings and the cultures of the peoples who lived there. The script on a ninth-century BC stele of Mesha from Dibon in Moab (the so-called "Moabite Stone") displays definite Hebrew characteristics, although the language is Moabite rather than Hebrew. (Moabite is a Canaanite dialect different in some respects from Hebrew). In later Moabite inscriptions (mainly seventh- and sixth-century seals), we find clearly Aramaic letters written alongside Hebrew letters and letters of a specific local character. Similar inscriptions bearing Edomite names were found in the vicinity of Elath and Umm el-Biyara near Petra. In the 9th century, Moabite (and Edomite) writing

Impressions of two Moabite seals

did not differ from the Hebrew script. But in the late 7th and 6th centuries BC, Aramaic elements began to intrude into these two scripts. The intrusion probably began in the last third of the 8th century BC. At that time, the political influence of Israel and Judah came to an end, and the Assyrians appeared on the King's Highway south of Damascus.

A ninth-century BC inscription from the Amman Citadel shows that the Ammonites spoke a Canaanite dialect similar to Hebrew and Moabite. But they adopted the Aramaic script from the Aramaeans who lived in Damascus. A number of Ammonite seals of the 7th century BC have been found which indicate that the Ammonites followed the Aramaic scribal tradition common in the Assyrian empire.

Impressions of two Ammonite seals

Aramaic was an official language of the Assyrian, Neo-Babylonian, and Persian empires. It was thus spoken and written in a vast area. Aramaic inscriptions have been found in Egypt. North Arabia, Palestine, Syria, Asia Minor, Mesopotamia, Persia, Afghanistan and Pakistan. Examination of these inscriptions has shown that no local script developed until the end of the 3rd century BC (about a hundred years after the fall of the Persian empire). During this time, the Official Aramaic script retained its uniform character.

Many nations used Aramaic as a second language and often it became the main spoken tongue. This also happened at a 5th century BC Jewish military colony in Elephantine. Over a hundred Aramaic papyri and ostraca were found there. These findings are our main source of knowledge of the Official Aramaic language and script. The writings consist of legal documents, private and official letters and two literary works. In the Persian period, an Aramaic lapidary script developed, intended for engraving on hard materials. But the influence of the speedier and more practical cursive hand was so strong that even many inscriptions on hard material were written in cursive writing. The lapidary script died out at the end of the 4th century BC. Standard

Left: Aramaic papyrus found at Elephantine

Above: A Palmyrene inscription

An Aramaic inscription from Hatra

Aramaic cursive, however, continued to be used for at least one hundred years after the fall of the Persian empire in 330 BC. Aramaic was widely spoken and written. It continued to flourish in the Hellenistic period, when Greek became the official language.

In the 3rd and 2nd centuries BC, local scripts began to branch out from the Aramaic. In the West, two national scripts were born: the Jewish ("square Hebrew") and the Nabataean. In the East, there were many offshoots: Palmyrene, Syriac, Mandaic, and other scripts as those of the inscriptions of Hatra (Mesopotamia), Nisa (Turkmenistan), Armazi (Georgia), Elymais (Khuzistan), etcetera. The Jewish book-

Right: Sumerian pictographic writing

Overleaf left: Assyrian cuneiform writing

Overleaf right: Egyptian hieroglyphic writing

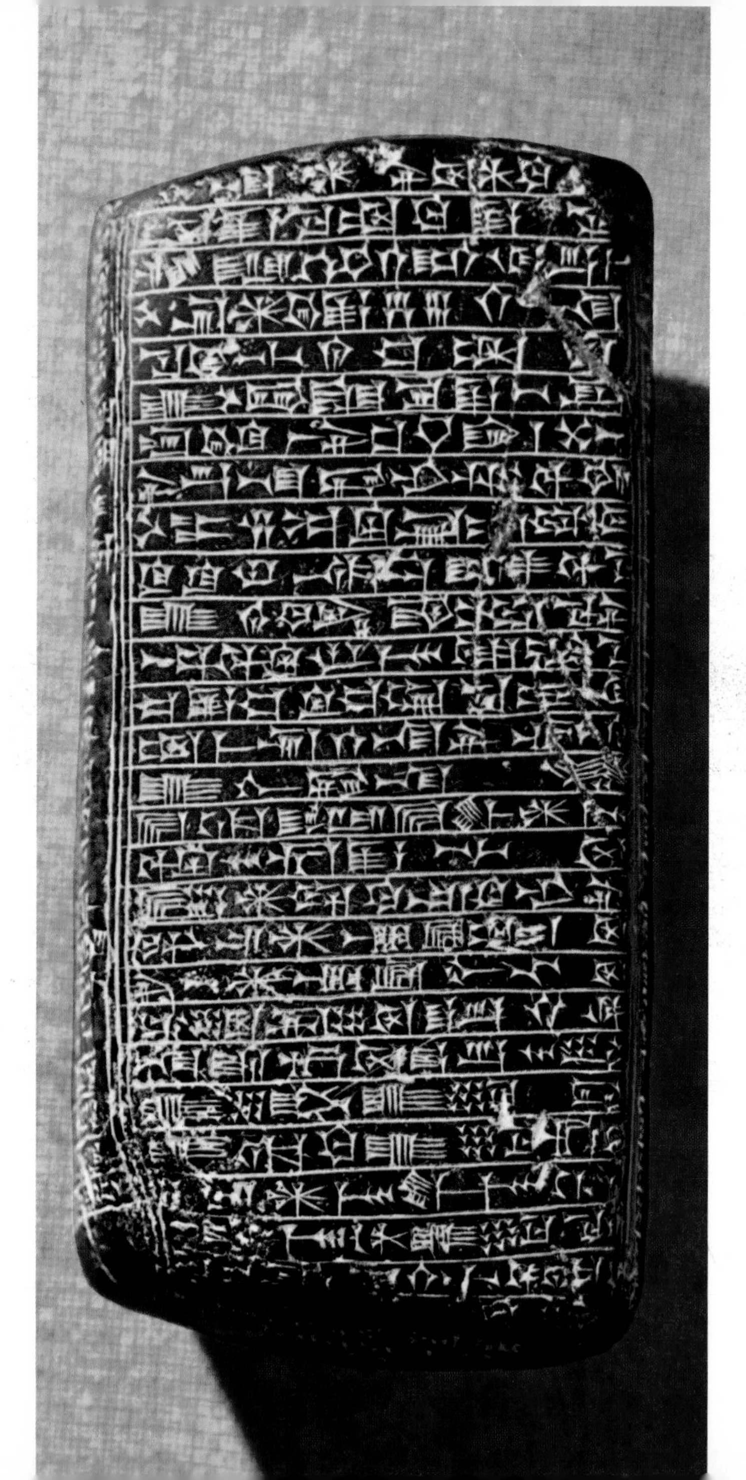

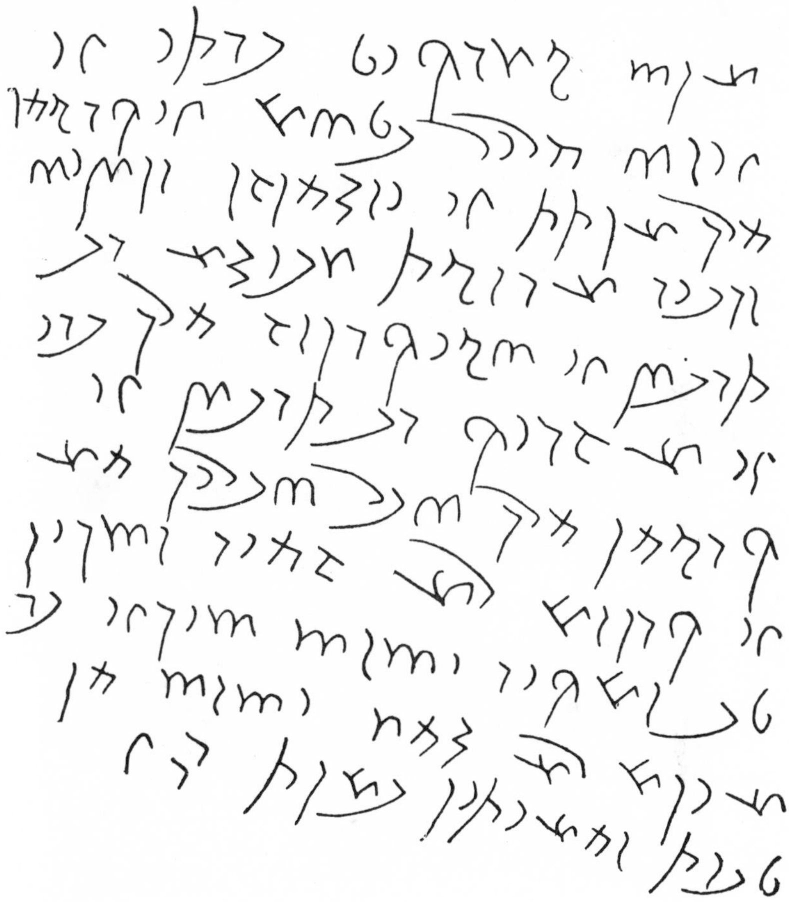

An Aramaic inscription from Armazi (Georgia, USSR)

hand became stabilized in the Herodian period. It has not undergone essential alterations since. The Arabic script developed from the Nabataean cursive hand. Although the eastern branches and their relationships to each other have not yet been thoroughly studied, the developments of some trends are quite clear. At Nisa, the Parthian capital, about 2000 ostraca of the 1st century BC have been found. Their script seems to be in a transitional stage between Official

Left: Eight-century BC Hebrew inscribed sherd

An Aramaic or early Parthian ostracon from Nisa (Turkmenistan, USSR)

Aramaic on the one hand and Parthian (Pahlavic), Persian (Parsic), Book-Pahlavi, and other scripts which were invented for writing Middle Iranian languages, on the other. The Aramaic script used by the Elymaeans is the ancestor of the Mandaic writing. (The Mandaeans are a religious sect living in Khuzistan near the Persian Gulf. They preserved an East Aramaic dialect resembling that of the Babylonian Talmud). The earliest Syriac inscriptions stem from the 1st and 2nd centuries AD. Their script resembles that of the contemporary cursive Palmyrene inscriptions. The Syriac script was employed by Christians in the northern part of Syria. There are three main Syriac

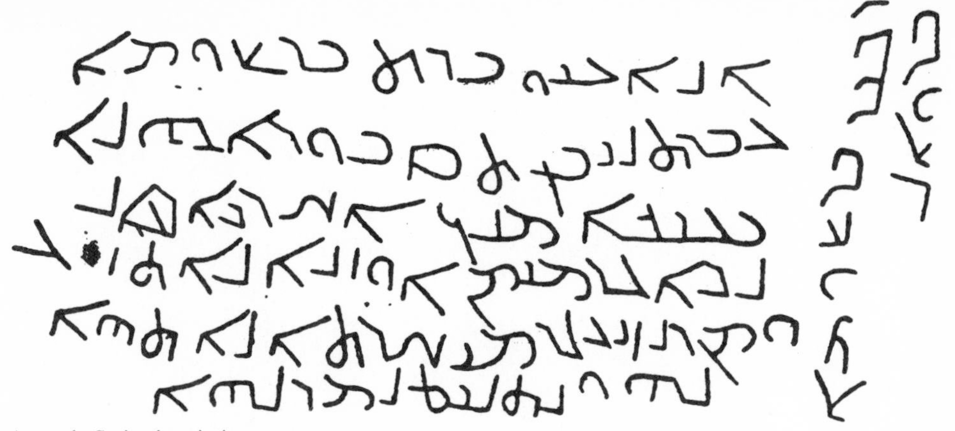

An early Syriac inscription

styles of writing: the *Estrangelo,* a formal script which resembles that of the early inscriptions; the *Serto,* a developed cursive ordinarily used by the Jacobites; and the *Nestorian,* another cursive variation. Syriac is an eastern Aramaic dialect spoken by the Christian communities in Edessa (modern Urfa in Southern Turkey) and in its vicinity. Although the Palestinian Christians spoke in a western Aramaic dialect, they adopted the Syriac script and wrote in a style similar to *Estrangelo*. The Manichaic script is an offshoot of the Palmyrene–Syriac branch. Mani, the founder of the Manichaean sect, invented this script in the 3rd century AD as a bookhand for writing religious manuscripts in a Middle Iranian dialect.

6. *The Jewish Script*

The Talmud ascribes the adoption of the Aramaic ("Assyrian") script to the time of Ezra, who may have brought it from the Babylonian Captivity. Aramaic script was also adopted in Judaea through the influence of the Babylonian and mainly the Persian administrations. At first it became the colloquial language of the educated classes and then spread to wider circles. It seems likely that in the Persian period, the Aramaic script was used for writing Aramaic text only. The earliest Hebrew manuscripts written in the Aramaic type of writing are fragments of Exodus and Samuel found in Qumran. These were probably written in the second half of the 3rd century BC in the Proto-Jewish script. This is the first evidence of the Jewish national development of the Official Aramaic script. From this period on, the Palaeo-Hebrew script was used mainly for Hebrew texts. The Jewish script was used both for Hebrew and Aramaic.

One of Bar Kochba's letters found at Wadi Murabba'at

The most important materials for studying the early evolution of the Jewish script are the Dead Sea Scrolls from the Qumran Caves and other documents from the caves of Wadi Murabba'at and Naḥal Ḥever. There are also tomb and ossuary inscriptions (mostly from Jerusalem) as well as some ostraca from Masada and Herodium. At Masada, a scroll of Ben-Sira was also discovered.

The Jewish script, like the Hebrew script, had no lapidary style. Monumental inscriptions were engraved in stone in the same formal script used to write the Bible on parchment scrolls.

Left: One of the Dead Sea scrolls

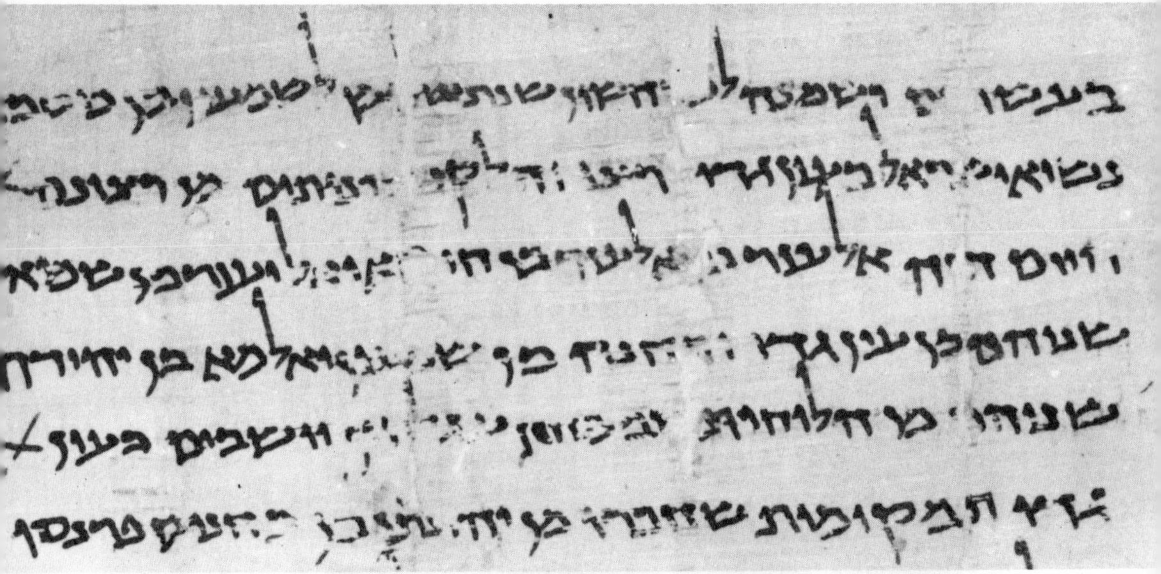

The top lines of a deed written on papyrus from Naḥal Ḥever

An example of this is the epitaph which indicates the burial place of "the bones of Uzziah, king of Judah". In addition to this formal bookhand, a cursive style evolved in the Herodian period. This flourished in the time of the Second Revolt (AD 132–5). Most of the messages sent by Bar Kochba to his officers were written on papyrus in this style. These were found in Naḥal Ḥever and Wadi Murabba'at. Soon after Bar Kochba's defeat, the cursive died out together with the Palaeo-Hebrew. But the Jewish bookhand continued to exist. The Jewish scribal tradition was already established at that time and became a religious practice,

The epitaph of Uzziah, king of Judah

which has survived till this day. For this reason, the Jewish bookhand, established mainly for writing the Torah, essentially preserved its ancient letter forms. An Israeli schoolboy today can read the two-thousand-year-old Dead Sea Scrolls almost without any difficulty.

7. *The Rise of the Arabic Script*

In the Persian period, the Edomites moved westward to Southern Judah and to the Negev. At the same time, an Arab tribe, the Nabataeans, began to invade Edom. Their native tongue was Arabic. We do not know if they brought some South Arabic type of writing with them from Arabia or if they were illiterate. But as they came into contact with other peoples in the area, they used Aramaic — the international script and language of that time. Diodorus Siculus tells us that the Nabataeans wrote a letter to Antigonus in 312 BC in Syrian (Aramaic) letters. At the same time as the Nabataeans conquered Edom, other Arab tribes settled in Palmyra, Hatra, and Edessa. Later, they established there independent kingdoms under Roman or Parthian suzerainty. In all of these centres, Aramaic was the written language. Thus, four scripts derived from Aramaic developed in this area. The Palmyrene and Hatran scripts died out when these oasis cities were destroyed. But the Syriac script of Edessa has survived among the Syriac Christians. The Nabataean script also continued to exist and eventually evolved into the Arabic writing.

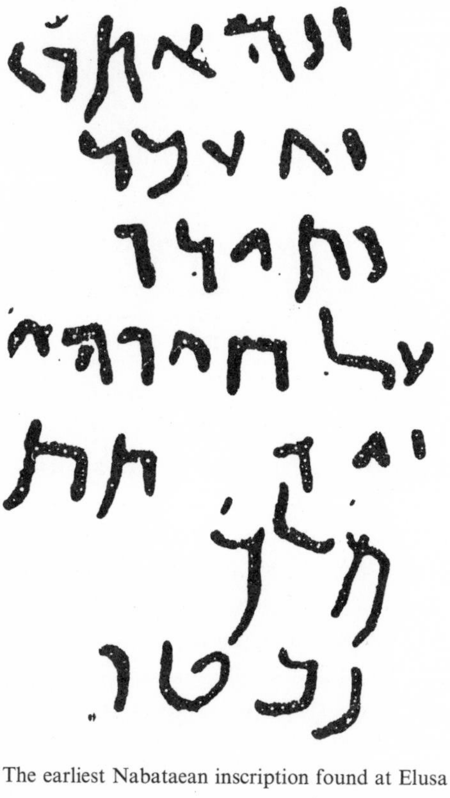

The earliest Nabataean inscription was found at Elusa in the Negev. It mentions "Ḥaretat (Aretas), king of the Nabataeans". This script is more like the Official Aramaic writing of the Persian period than the later Nabataean

The earliest Nabataean inscription found at Elusa

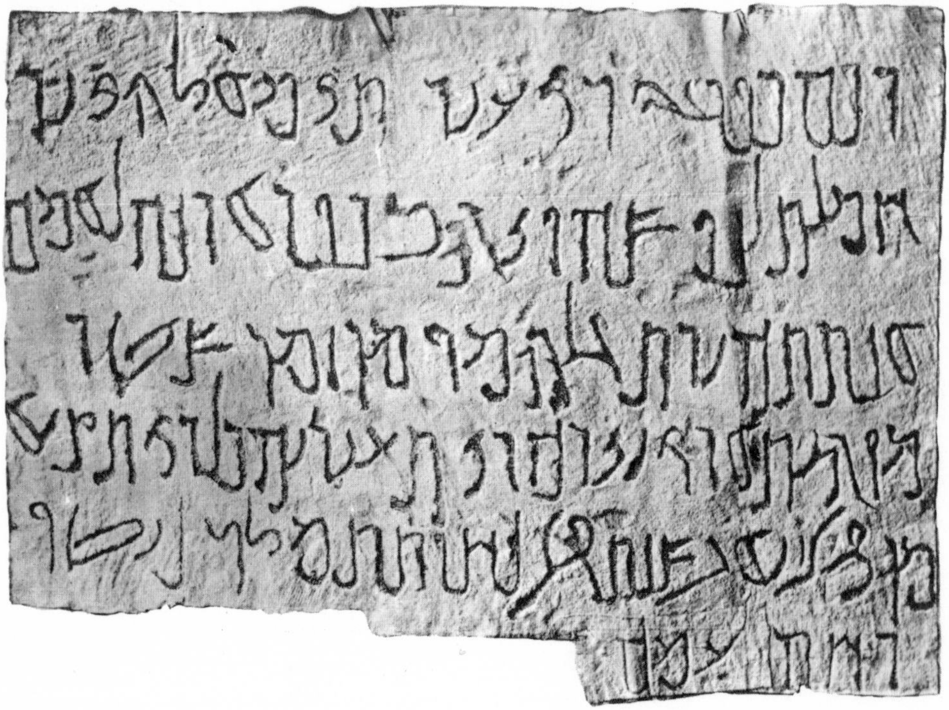

Monumental Nabataean inscription

inscriptions. This indicates an early date, and the king seems to be Aretas I. He is mentioned in the First Book of Maccabees as the Nabataean ruler to whom the former high priest Jason fled in 169 BC. Other Nabataean inscriptions, many of which are dated, clearly exhibit Nabataean letter forms. Nabataean inscriptions were found in the capital, Petra, and in other Nabataean towns in Transjordan and the Negev, as well as in Egypt, North Arabia, and even Italy. These are mostly burial and votive inscriptions. In AD 106, the Romans annexed the Nabataean Kingdom and established a province called Arabia. Until that date, coins were struck with Nabataean legends. Written material in Nabataean consists after AD 106 of inscriptions from Northern Arabia and thousands of graffiti (from the 2nd and 3rd centuries) which have been found in the Sinai. But the most important contributions to the

Earliest Arabic inscriptions. *Above:* The Namara inscription, AD 328. *Below:* An inscription dated AD 568

development of the Nabataean cursive and to the pre-history of the Arabic script are some dated Nabataean papyri. These writings, from the time of Rabel II (the last Nabataean king) and later, until AD 135, were found in one of the Judaean Desert caves in the Ḥever Valley together with Jewish documents of that time.

In the Nabataean Inscriptions and documents the language is Aramaic. But there are some Arabic words and linguistic forms, as well as Arabic proper names. The number of Arabic characteristics grew as times went on. In an inscription from 328 found at Namara, the script is still Nabataean but the language is entirely Arabic. In three sixth-century inscriptions found in Syria (two of them dated to 512 and 568) the scripts are more Arabic than Nabataean. They have some resemblance to the early Arabic style developed in al-Kufa. The Kufic script was used

Arabic inscriptions. *Above:* Early 10th century AD (Kufic style of writing). *Below:* Late 13th century AD

in the early Islamic period mainly for writing on stone. The most common Arabic style is the Naskhi, which came into common use in the eleventh century for copying manuscripts. It is widely used today both for copying the Quran (the Moslem Holy Scripture) and for secular writing.

In the cursive Nabataean documents from the 'Cave of Letters' in the Ḥever Valley there is already a tendency to assimilate certain letters: *bet* and *nun; gimel* and *ḥet; zayin* and *resh; yod* and *taw; pe* and *qof*. Because of this evolution, the reader of early Arabic writing had to distinguish between various letters from the context alone. Also, the Arabic language is richer in consonant sounds than the Aramaic. The Arab writers had to express 28 consonants with the 22 letters which existed in the Aramaic–Nabataean script. In order to make reading easier, they introduced marks which differentiate between the various sounds: ج *(jim)*, ح *(ḥa)*, and خ *(ḫa)*; ر *(ra)* and ز *(za)*; د *(dal)* and ذ *(ḏal)*, etcetera.

The West Semitic alphabetic order appears in the 14th century BC (in Ugarit) and was later on adopted with a few changes in Greek and Latin. But the Arabic alphabetical order is different. It seems to be based on the similarities between the letter-forms and that of the sounds of the various signs. (The Ethiopic alphabet has yet another order). In Arabic, the 22 letters in the Aramaic or Hebrew order of the alphabet was employed for numerical values. As in Hebrew the letters *alef* to *taw* designated the numbers 1 to 400. The six additional Arabic consonantal signs indicate 500, 600, etcetera, jumping by 100's to 1000.

8. *The Antiquity of the Greek Alphabet*

In the 2nd millennium BC, the Minoans and the Mycenaeans achieved civilizations of quite a high level. They developed both pictographic and linear scripts. Of these scripts, only one of the linear ones is understood today. Michael Ventris deciphered Linear B in 1953, proving that it was a syllabic writing system practised by Greek-speaking Mycenaeans. The Mycenaean Greeks, who lived in Cyprus, preserved their syllabic script until the later part of the 1st millennium BC. But Linear B died out with the Mycenaean civilization which was destroyed by the Doric invasion about 1100 BC. The period following this destruction is known as a Dark Age in the history of Greece. Until the late 9th and even the 8th centuries BC, there are no indications of any close contact between the Greeks and the peoples who lived on the eastern shore of the Mediterranean and wrote

Left and above: One of the earliest archaic Greek inscriptions on a vase found at Athens, 8th century BC

in an alphabetic script. We can suppose, however, that even before this Canaanite traders visited the Greek islands.

Since ancient times, scholars have agreed that the Greek alphabet had West Semitic origins. But they still cannot agree about the time of the earliest use of the alphabet among the Greeks. The oldest archaic Greek inscriptions known today belong to the 8th century BC. These are legends on vases from Athens and Mount Hymettos or sherds from Corinth, and rock-cut inscriptions from Thera. There are local variations in the scripts of these and other archaic Greek inscriptions. But all the local scripts had some common traits. They continued to exist

An archaic Greek inscription written in boustrophedon

until the 4th century BC, when the Ionian version of the script and the left-to-right direction was accepted generally. The Greeks used the 22 West Semitic letters. Some of these letters designated vowels, which in itself constitutes a most important innovation. In the archaic Greek alphabet five supplementary letters were added: **Υ, Φ, Χ, Ψ, Ω**. The style of writing was lapidary. The direction of writing and the profiles of the letters kept changing. The archaic Greeks wrote in horizontal lines, either from right to left, or from left to right, or in horizontal *boustrophedon,* where the writing runs from right to left and from left to right on alternate lines.

Today, many scholars believe that the

An early sixth-century BC inscription on a decorated vase from Corinth

Greeks adopted the Phoenician script in the 8th century BC. Rhys Carpenter said that this idea "grows every year more formidable and more conclusive" because no inscriptions have been found earlier than the 8th century. Others believe that it took a long time for the Greeks to change from the West Semitic letter forms and to improve upon the Semitic system by adding vowel signs. It is assumed that before the 8th century BC there existed an earlier Greek alphabet which was closer to the West Semitic, and that the archaic Greek script as found on the earliest known inscriptions had already undergone many changes. This problem is important for understanding the cultural history of archaic Greece. Did Greece have a long period of illiteracy after the Linear B script died out with the Mycenaean civilization?

The fact that no inscriptions earlier than 8th century BC have been found cannot be considered conclusive evidence. We know that the Hebrews adopted the alphabet in the 12th or 11th century BC, but only one Hebrew inscription — the Gezer calendar — has been found which is earlier than 8th century BC. The Aramaeans began to use the alphabet shortly after the Hebrews, but there are only a few inscriptions from the 9th century BC. But beginning with the 8th century, the number of Hebrew and Aramaic inscriptions gradually increases. The Hebrew, Aramaic, and archaic Greek material seem to indicate that the knowledge of writing began to be widely distributed in the 8th century BC.

From the second half of the 11th century BC onwards the Phoenician script was written from right to left. At that time, and during the following century, the shapes of the letters were stabilized. Until the 8th century BC, Phoenician script developed toward cursiveness. The archaic Greek writing was lapidary, and almost pictographical. The direction of writing and the profiles of the letters were not yet stabilized. It is difficult to believe that the Greeks adopted a developed script and turned it into a more primitive one. We should consider, therefore, that some Greeks might have learned the Proto-Canaanite script when Canaanite merchants visited the Greek islands or the Greek mainland during the late 12th or early 11th century BC. At that stage, the Proto-Canaanite alphabet had been reduced to twenty-two letters. Some of these still preserved their pictographic forms. They were written in lines from right to left or left to right and sometimes in horizontal *boustrophedon*. Most of the archaic Greek letter-forms resemble the West Semitic letters as they looked about 1100 BC. There is special

Classical Greek formal writing

resemblance in I (Z), ⊟ (H), M (M), ⊙ (O) and Σ (S). There is, however, one Greek letter which could not have been taken over from the eleventh-century Proto-Canaanite but seems to have come from the ninth-century Phoenician script. This is the *kappa* (K), whose West Semitic equivalent — the *kaf* — was written (Ψ) until the late 10th century BC. But the exact reproduction of eleventh-century BC *kaf* — Ψ — appears as a supplementary letter designating *khi* in the Western Greek local scripts. It is possible that this letter, shaped like three fingers, served in the 11th and 10th centuries as both *k* and *kh*. When the Greeks wanted to distinguish between these two sounds, they borrowed the contemporary Phoenician *kaf* — Ƴ — which in the meantime had developed a downward stroke. It seems likely also that one other letter was adopted from the Phoenician script later than the 11th century BC. This is the Y, which appears in the Greek alphabetical order after T. Y is the first Greek additional letter. The archaic Greeks used the Proto-Canaanite *waw* (Greek *vau*) just as the Semites did for the consonant *w*. Later, in the 10th or 9th century BC, the Greek *vau* changed its shape and turned into ϝ. When the Greeks invented their vowel system and needed a sign for *u*, they looked for a Phoenician model. They found the contemporary *waw* quite suitable. Since the Greeks were always aware of the origin of their script, whenever they needed supplementary letters, they looked first of all for Phoenician prototypes.

The most important Greek innovation was as we have noted the invention of the vowel-signs. They changed the values of certain Semitic letters not used in Greek and turned them into vowels. The *aleph* became an *A (alpha)*, *he* was turned into *E (epsilon)*, *yod* into *I (iota)*, and *'ayin* into *O (omicron)*. Since *waw* in archaic Greek had turned into ϝ and was a consonant, *Y*, the Greek letter designating *u*, is among the supplementary letters. The Greeks followed the Semitic invention of the alphabetic system in the middle of the second millennium with the introduction of vowel signs about five hundred years later. This was a further step towards the simplification of writing which put literacy in everyone's reach.

9. *The Early Evolution of the Latin Alphabet*

The most important derivative of archaic Greek script is the Latin or Roman alphabet. This system of writing has played a most important role in the history of civilization.

The earliest Latin inscriptions come

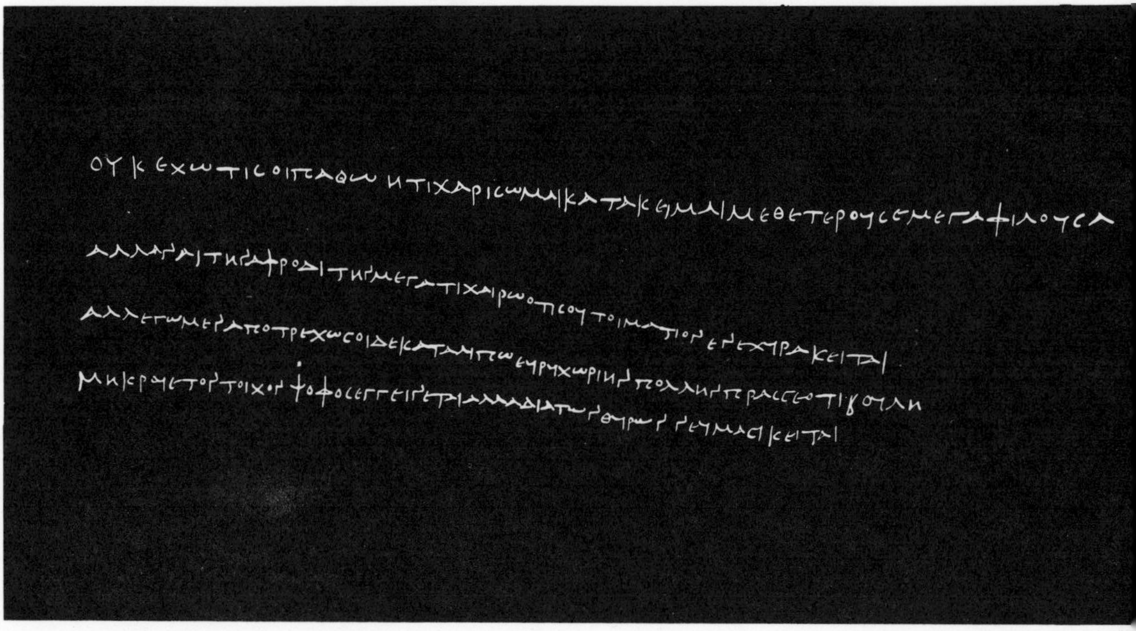

Classical Greek cursive writing

from the 7th to 6th centuries BC. These were found on a *fibula* (brooch) at Praeneste, a tombstone from the Roman Forum, and on the inscribed Duenos vase. These inscriptions were written either in right-to-left direction or in *boustrophedon*.

The Latin alphabet did not use all the archaic Greek letters. The archaic Greek local scripts were used by mainland, island, and colonial Greeks, as well as by people who did not speak Greek at all. These were the Phrygians, Lydians, Lycians, Carians, etcetera, in Asia Minor, and certain Italian peoples like the Etruscans, Umbrians, Oscians, and Romans. When different peoples adopted the scripts, they accepted or rejected certain signs according to the requirements of their particular languages.

The archaic Greek alphabet consisted of 27 letters. It used the 22 original Semitic signs plus 5 supplementary letters. Classical Greek (the Ionian local script universally accepted from the 4th century onwards), omitted three letters: *vau* (or *digamma), san* and *qoppa*. In

Etruscan abecedary on a school tablet found at Marsiliana

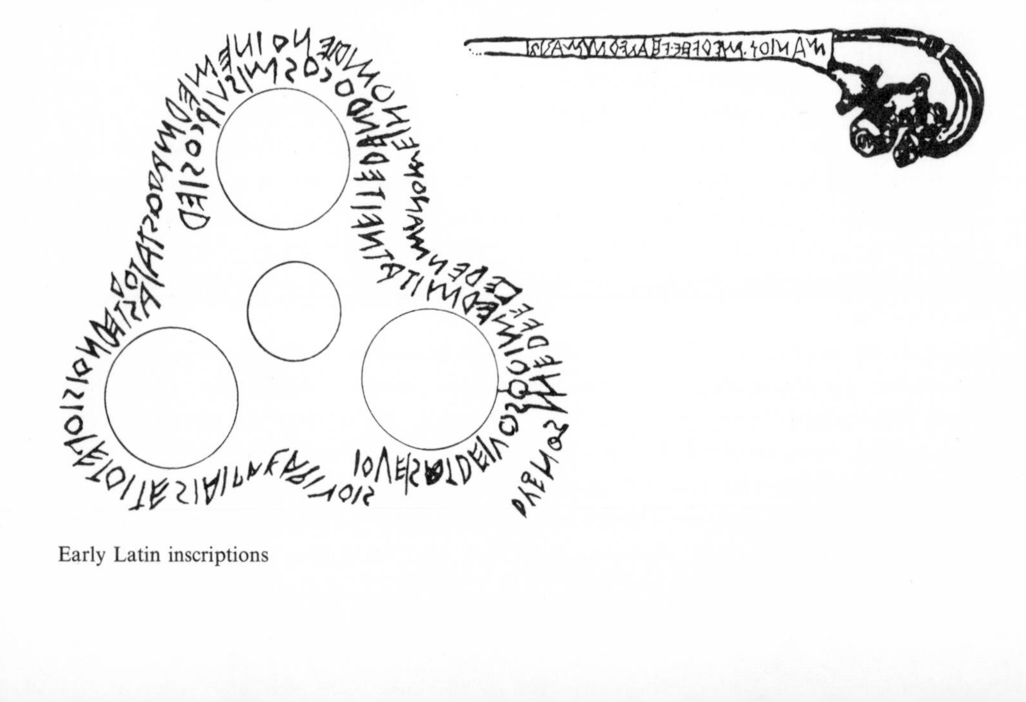

Early Latin inscriptions

the Greek alphabetic numeral system, *vau* has been preserved and stands for the number 6. *San* has been omitted, and *qoppa* stands for 90. (In Hebrew, *ṣade* = 90, *qof* = 100).

The Latin alphabet adopted the archaic Greek local script as used in the Chalcidian Greek colonies in Italy, by the way of the Etruscans. The Etruscans had no *g* among the sounds of their language and then used the letter *gamma* (ᐸ,C) to express the sound *k*.In the Latin alphabet the *zeta* was omitted. In place of the *zeta,* the seventh letter in the alphabet, they used a new letter to indicate *g*. This letter was created by adding a bar to the lower part of the crescent letter C (C–G). In addition to the *zeta* other archaic Greek letters also were omitted from the alphabet when it was adopted by the Romans. These were *theta,* the older form of *ksi, san* and all the Greek supplementary letters except *ypsilon.* K still had a place in the Latin alphabet, but its use was very much restricted. Since the same sound could be expressed by C and Q, K was used only in a limited number of words like *Kalendae. Ypsilon* — whose form was V — was used for both *u* and *v,* just as *iota* (I) stood for both a vowel and a consonant. In the time of Quintilian (second half of the 1st century AD), X was the last letter and closed the alphabet. But after the Romans conquered Greece, the Latin language began to borrow Greek words. Some of these contained the letters Y and Z. Therefore, in the time of Cicero, these above mentioned letters were added to the Latin alphabet and Z became its last letter.

In the Roman period, the Latin alphabet consisted of 23 letters. Today there are 26 letters due to the invention of J, U, and W. J is used to distinguish between the signs for the vowel *i* and the consonant *y*. U is used for the vowel sound *u* to distinguish it from the consonant *v*. J and U were added in the early Middle Ages. W came later in the 11th century AD.

The Latin script was used for writing most of the European languages. Although languages change constantly, the written form is usually more formal and more conservative. The spoken language may change, but writers do not mind if the written word does not correspond exactly to its spoken form. The ideal phonetic alphabet would have only one letter for each speech sound and one sound for each letter. But the great languages of civilization, such as English and French, have difficulties with exact spelling. One of these difficulties stems from the fact that the languages are split into many dialects, with different pronunciations for the same word. It would be very difficult

Latin inscription from Caesarea, Roman period

to write every dialect in its exact form, because the language would then have no unity. Therefore, some words must be written inexactly.

But bad as English spelling may be, it still retains most of the principles of alphabetic writing. It takes only a year or two of study to learn to spell English. The Chinese, on the other hand, have to devote many years to learning characters if they are to have a complete command of their literature.

SECTION TWO

DEVELOPMENT OF THE LETTERS

A

The initial letters of the various alphabets used today are the Hebrew א *('alef)*, Arabic ا *('alīf)*, Greek Α *(alpha)* and Latin A. All of these developed from a common ancestor. This early ancestor appears first in the Proto-Sinaitic inscriptions of about 1500 BC. It was drawn as a picture of an ox-head [ox-head sign]. Its name was probably *'alp*. *'Alp* is a Canaanite word which corresponds to the Hebrew word *'alūf*, meaning "ox". The value of the letter was not the entire word *'alp*, but only its first sound. This means that the picture had an acrophonic value. The picture of *'alp* [ox-head sign] symbolized the sound ', a consonant which does not exist in the European languages.

The pictorial shape of [ox-head sign] has changed with time. In the second half of the second millennium, the following developments can be followed in the Proto-Canaanite script [ox-head sign]→[sign]→[sign]. At about 1000 BC, we find the classical form of the early Phoenician *'alef* 𐤀.

Another form which developed from the pictographic [ox-head sign] is the South Arabic and Ethiopic *'alef*. This offshoot began to develop about 1300 BC in the following way: [sign]→[sign]. This finally yielded the Ethiopic አ, which is used today.

When the Greeks learned the Proto-Canaanite alphabet about 1100 BC, the stance of the *'alef* had not yet been stabilized. In archaic Greek inscriptions from the 8th and 7th centuries BC, we find three rotations of the *alpha*. One is similar to the Phoenician *'alef* , and others are in different positions, such as or . This last form became finally accepted by all the Greek local scripts. All the non-Greeks who adopted the alphabet, including the Romans, also used this position. So A became the first letter of the Latin alphabet.

But the Greeks did not need this letter to designate the consonant ' which appeared only in the Semitic languages. Therefore, they used the *alpha* as a sign for the vowel *a*.

The (ancient) Hebrew *'alef* used in the period of the First Temple developed from the early Phoenician in the way: → → → . The latter shape is the formal Hebrew *'alef* of the late 7th or early 6th century BC. It survived in the Dead Sea Scrolls which were written in old Hebrew characters in the time of the Hasmonaeans and in Jewish coin legends . This *'alef* evolved into the Samaritan which is used even today.

The Aramaic *'alef* is another offshoot of the early Phoenician. It developed in the 7th and 6th centuries BC in the following way: → → → . In the 5th century BC it reached its classical form which has been preserved by the Jewish (square Hebrew) script. In the Jewish script, the left leg of the letter had become long and straight. In the Dead Sea Scrolls, it already appears as which is essentially the *'alef* of the modern Hebrew alphabet.

The Aramaic developed in the Nabataean branch as follows

→ → → → → |. This last cursive *'alef* occurs already in the late first-century AD Nabataean deeds found at the Ḥever Valley near the Dead Sea. It indicates the date when the form of the Arabic *'alīf* — | became fixed.

B

The common ancestor of the Hebrew ב, Arabic ب, and Greek and Latin B was a pictograph designating a house . The Canaanite word for house is *bēt,* and this word is still in use as the name of the second letter of the Hebrew alphabet. Again, the principle is acrophonic: the letter stands for only the first sound of the word. Therefore, the value is b. The Greeks called this letter *beta.*

In South Arabic, its shape was ; in Ethiopic . In the Proto-Canaanite script, the letter developed as follows: → → → . The basic shape of this last form survived in the Phoenician (,), Hebrew (,) and Samaritan ( ) scripts. In the archaic Greek local alphabets there were several variants of *beta:* (, 8, , ,), but 8 prevailed. When writing was stabilized in a left-to-right direction, the rightward profile B became universally accepted.

The Aramaic *bet* (like *dalet, resh,* and *'ayin*) already has an open top in the late 8th century BC, . In the 5th century BC, its form is . From the 4th century BC onwards, the downstroke is a vertical curving into a horizontal base. There is also a tendency to straighten the top of the letter . In the early Jewish script the tick on the left side of the top is the only remnant of the half-circle head. In the Herodian period, the base of the Jewish *bet* is occasionally written with a separate left-to-right stroke ב. This fashion prevails and becomes common in the Jewish bookhand. The Jewish *bet* does not change its basic shape through the ages. It is essentially identical to the modern Hebrew ב.

The Nabataean *bet* loses its top) and the new form is adopted for the Arabic *ba*. However, other Nabataean letters evolved into similar forms, so diacritic (distinguishing) marks had to be added in order to distinguish ﺑ *(ba)*, from ﺗ *(ta)*, ﻧ *(nun)* and ﻳ *(ya)* in medial positions.

C

The third letter of the Latin alphabet is C. In the Hebrew and Greek alphabets, however, the third letters are respectively *gimel* ג and *gamma* Γ, which correspond to the sound *g*.

The basic shape of the Proto-Canaanite *gimel* consisted of two strokes forming an angle. In the Proto-Sinaitic inscriptions we find L, in the Proto-Canaanite ˥ or ∧. In the archaic Greek local scripts, the *gamma* could be drawn either Λ or ˥ or >. The classical Greek preserved the second eastern archaic form in rightward profile Γ. But the Latin alphabet adopted the Western variant of the *gamma* < which turned into C. The Etruscans had no *g* among the sounds of their language, and so they used the *gamma* for the sound *k*. Since the Romans learned the Greek alphabet from the Etruscans, the change of value of this letter sound from *g* into *k* is obvious (See below G).

In the 10th century BC, the Phoenician *gimel* could be written either ˥ or ∧. The first type was adopted by the ancient Hebrew script. The second prevailed in the later Phoenician and Aramaic scripts. The Jewish *gimel* developed from Aramaic ∧ as follows: λ → λ → ⅄. The latter corresponds to the square Hebrew ג.

The Arabic *jim* ﺟ (in final position ج) developed from the Nabataean ⅄ → ⅄. But diacritic marks had to be added in order to distinguish this letter *(jim,* Egyptian Arabic *gim)* from *ḥa* and *ḫa*, which had evolved a similar shape; *jim* = ج; *ḥa* = ح; *ḫa* = خ.

D

The earliest common ancestor of the Hebrew ד, *(dalet),* Arabic د *(dal),* and the Latin D appears in the Proto-Sinaitic inscriptions as a pictograph designating a fish (in Hebrew *"dag"*) ⊳◇. This developed in the South Arabic writing into ⊳|. In the Proto-Canaanite script, the picture of the fish turned into a triangle ◁. This triangle survived in the *delta* (the Greek letter D) of the eastern archaic Greek local scripts Δ and hence in Greek classical writing, where it is written Δ. In the western archaic Greek scripts, the triangle was turned to its side ▷, and later developed into D. This last form was adopted by the Latin script for D.

In the early Phoenician writing, the *dalet* was still written like the Proto-Canaanite ◁, which we have mentioned above. But later, the left angle became curved and the right stroke developed a downward tail ◁. In the Hebrew *dalet,* the upper stroke was also drawn leftwards ◁ and so was the Samaritan ◁.

In the Semitic fluent cursive writings, however, there is a

tendency to avoid closed circles. For this reason, the Phoenician cursive opens the head of the *dalet* at its lower part 𐤃 and the Aramaic script opens the top of the letter 𐡃 → 𐡃 → 𐡃. The *dalet* is very similar in form to the *resh* (the letter for R). It happens that both letters are written the same way. In Syriac, only distinguishing marks differentiate between *dalet* (ܕ) and *resh* (ܪ). The form of the Jewish *dalet* in the Herodian period *(ca.* 30 BC–AD 70) was 𐡃, from which the modern square Hebrew *dalet* ד developed. This form emphasizes the right upper angle in order to distinguish it from *resh* (ר).

The Nabataean cursive *dalet* turned into a single stroke I. The *resh* evolved into a similar shape. The late Nabataean *dalet,* and mainly the Arabic *dal* were written in an angular way 〉. In the Arabic script, this letter was used both for *dal* د and for *ḏal* ذ. The distinguishing mark was added to designate the sound *ḏ.* which had no specific mark in the Aramaic and Nabataean scripts.

E

The fifth letter of the Latin alphabet is E and its counterpart in the Hebrew alphabet is ה *(he)*. Both stem from a pictograph which dates to about 1500 BC, representing a calling (or praying) figure 𓀠, 𓀠. In the South Arabic script, the figure developed into 𐩠, and in Proto-Canaanite writing it turned into 𐤄. The Greek and Latin alphabets basically preserved this latter form, but they turned it to the right, E. In Semitic writing, the value of the letter is the consonant *h*. The Greeks, on the other hand, turned it into the vowel *e*.

The Hebrew name of the letter is *he,* with a pronounced *h* sound, and the Greek name is *epsilon.*

The Phoenician alphabet basically preserved the late Proto-Canaanite form of the letter . This developed into the Hebrew and the Samaritan .

In Aramaic, the *he* joined the two lower horizontal bars into one vertical stroke and it was written . This form was adopted by the Jewish script , but later the left vertical separated from the upper horizontal stroke. From this, the modern Hebrew *he,* written ה, evolved.

The Nabataean *he* joined the two downstrokes and thus the Arabic ه *(ha)* developed.

F

The sixth letter of the Latin alphabet is F. In the Hebrew alphabet, however, the sixth letter ו *–waw–* corresponds to the sound *w*. In classical Greek, this letter does not occur at all. In archaic Greek script, however, it existed in the form of (named *vau* or *digamma*). The letter later became a numeral designating 6 and having the form .

At about 1500 BC, Proto-Sinaitic and Proto-Canaanite inscriptions used the letter in a form which resembled a mace or a peg (the Hebrew word for peg is *waw*). Later, the circular top of the letter opened up and in the 10th century BC, the letter was written in two varying forms: the Y-shaped *waw* and the *waw* which was shaped like the number 4, . The first form (Y-shaped) was accepted in the

Hebrew script and was written 𐤅 → 𐤅 → 𐤅 → 𐤅. In Samaritan, the letter was written ࠅ. The Phoenician and Aramaic scripts, however, adopted the 4-shaped *waw*. In the Phoenician script, it developed 𐤅 → 𐤅 → 𐤅 and in the Aramaic 𐡅 → 𐡅 → 𐡅 → 𐡅. The Nabataean *waw* closed its top 𐢈 and hence the Arabic و evolved. The Jewish *waw* ו → ו basically preserved the Aramaic shape of the letter.

The Phoenician *waw* is the ancestor of four Latin letters, F, U, V and Y. The consonant F developed from the archaic Greek *vau* and U-V were derived from the Greek vowel *ypsilon,* which is the first of the five letters that the Greeks added to their alphabet. (See below U, V and Y.)

G

The seventh letter of the Latin alphabet is G. In the Hebrew alphabet, however, the seventh letter is *zayin,* which corresponds to the Greek *zeta,* the ancestor of the Latin Z. (See below Z.)

The Latin G developed from C. In the western archaic Greek local scripts, the *gamma* was written not as Γ, but as < or C. Since the Etruscans had no *g* among the sounds of their language, they used the *gamma* <-C for the sound *k*. But the Romans had a *g* in their phonemic system, so they added a small bar to the C and thus G came to designate *g*. There was no *z* in the original Latin language, so they placed the G in the place of the Greek *zeta*. (For the Semitic letters designating *g* see above, C.)

H

The Latin H, the Hebrew ח *(ḥet),* and the Arabic ح *(ḥa)* developed from the early Proto-Canaanite pictograph of a fence 𐤇, 𐤇. In the later Proto-Canaanite script, the *ḥet* had the shape of a box with an inner horizontal bar 𐤇. This form survived in the archaic Greek script, and then it developed into H, which was adopted also in the Latin alphabet. The archaic Greeks did not use it as the Semites did for the consonant *ḥ (ḥet)*, but for *h (heta)*. Later, the Greeks turned it into the vowel *(eta),* which is a long *e* as opposed to the *epsilon* which is a short *e*. The sound *h,* which is roughly breathed (aspirated) before a vowel at the beginning of a word is marked by ʿ. In the Latin alphabet, however, H is a consonant.

The Phoenician script preserved the older form of the letter, but the vertical strokes were somewhat elongated 𐤇. Also in Hebrew, it is written 𐤇 (or sometimes 𐤇), and in Samaritan 𐤇. The Aramaic *ḥet* dropped two of the horizontal bars as early as the late 8th century BC, and the letter became ח. This is the basic form of the modern Hebrew ח.

The Arabic حـ (in final position ح) developed through the Nabataean as follows: → → → → . In the Arabic phonemic system, there is another sound besides the *ḥa,* the *ḫa,* which had no sign in the Aramaic and Nabataean alphabet. (These alphabets each consisted of 22 letters.) The *ḫa* was marked by a diacritic (distinguishing) mark on the top of the letter خ. The same letter with a diacritic mark on its lower part ج designated *jim*. (For the *jim* see above C.)

I

The earliest common ancestor of the Latin I, Hebrew י *(yod)* and Arabic ي *(ya)* was the pictograph of a hand (in Hebrew *yad*) with its forearm: ⌙, ⅃. In the 11th and 10th centuries BC, the *yod* developed into 𐤉, which basically did not change in the Hebrew (𐤉, 𐤉, 𐤉), Samaritan (ࠉ) and Phoenician (𐤉, 𐤉) scripts. However, the Aramaic cursive reduced it as follows: 𐡉 → 𐡉 → 𐡉 → 𐡉 → 𐡉. In the fourth and third centuries BC, two varying forms evolved. One resembles the numeral "2" ⋜, and the other has an inverted v-form ^. While the Nabataean developed the 2-shaped *yod* 𐢍 which turned into the Arabic *ya* ي, the Jewish script adopted the inverted v-shape and preserved the small size of the letter י (in order to distinguish between it and the longer *waw*). This developed into י.

From the eleventh-century Proto-Canaanite *yod* 𐤉, the archaic Greek *iota* developed as follows: ϟ → ϟ → |. It was used for designating both the vowel *i* and the consonant *y* (when it stood before or after another vowel). In the Latin alphabet, the I was used in the same way, until in the Middle Ages a new form J began to replace the consonantal I.

Right: Illustrated Jewish manuscript dated *ca.* AD 1300
Overleaf left: A thirteenth-century AD illustrated Arabic manuscript
Overleaf right: Fifteenth-century illustrated Latin manuscript

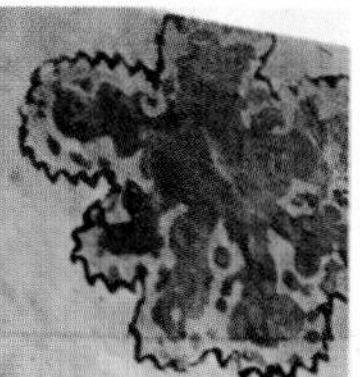

לחצינו"

ונצעק אל יי' אלה''

אבותינו כמה

שנ' ויהי בימים הרבים ההם

וימת מלך מצרים ויאנחו

בני ישר' מן העבודה ויזע'

ויזעקו ותעל שועתם אל

האלהים מן העבודה"

וישמע יי' את קולנו

כמה שנ' וישמע

אלהים את נאקתם ויזכור

אלהים את בריתו את אברהם

٣٤
تسلط علي بغيا واجعل لي من لدنك سلطانا نصيرا اللهم احرسني بعينك وعونك
واخصصني بأمنك ومنك وتولني باختيارك وخيرك ولا تكلني إلى كلاءة غيرك

Orbis situ
dicere aggredior
impeditu opus
et facundie
minime ca
pax. Costat
enim fere ge
tiu locoru
nominibus et eoru
perplexo sa
tis ordine que
psequi longa e
magis qua beni
gna materia. Veru
aspici tn cognosciq3
dignissimu. et quod
sine ope ingenij ora
tis ac ipsa sui con
teplatione preciu ope
attendentiu absoluat. Dicam tn alias plura et exactius
nunc aut ut queq3 sunt clarissima et strictim. Ac primo
quide q sit forma totius q maxime partes q singule modo
sint ut q habitentur expediam. Deinde rursus oras omni
et litora ut intra extra q sint atq3 ut ea subit ac cir
cumfluit pelagus additis q i natura regionu incolaru me
moranda sunt. Id q facilius sciri possit atq3 accipi paulo al
tius summa repetetur. Omne igitur hoc quicquid est cui mu
di celi q nomen indidimus unu id est

ΑΡΣΙΝΟΗΣ
ΦΙΛΑΔΕΛΦΟΥ
Κ

J

Compared to the involved developments of the other letters, the history of J is relatively very short. It was introduced only in the Middle Ages in order to distinguish in the Latin writing between the consonantal *i* and the vowel *i*. (See above I and below U.)

K

A pictograph of the palm of the hand Ѱ was the source for the Latin K, Hebrew כ *(kaf)* and Arabic ك *(kaf)*. This shape appears as early as 1500 BC both in the Proto-Sinaitic inscriptions and on an inscribed potsherd from Gezer. The Hebrew name of the letter, *kaf* (the word which means "palm" in Hebrew), still preserves the idea of the original form of the letter.

In the later Proto-Canaanite and in the early Phoenician scripts, the letter was represented by three fingers stemming from a common base Ψ. From the late 10th century BC and onwards, a downstroke was added, 𐤊.

The *kaf* developed in the various West Semitic branches as follows: 𐤊 → 𐤊 → 𐤊 → 𐤊 (Phoenician); 𐤊 → 𐤊 → 𐤊 (Hebrew); 𐤊 (Samaritan); 𐤊 → 𐤊 → 𐤊 (Aramaic). From the 4th century BC, the Aramaic *kaf* (as the other letters with long downstrokes, namely *mem, nun, pe* and *ṣade)* developed distinctive final and medial forms. (In certain Semitic scripts, some letters have different forms in different positions in the words.) In the middle of the word the downstrokes were bent to the

Left: Greek inscription on a gold coin of Arsinoe, daughter of Ptolemais I, king of Egypt (316–269 BC)

left towards the next letter within the word. In final position the long downstrokes were preserved. This distinction led to the early Jewish medial *kaf* כ and final *kaf* ך, as well as the Modern Hebrew medial כ and final ך.

The Arabic *kaf* also has different forms when it is used in the middle ـكـ and at the end ك of a word. These developed from the Nabataean *kaf,* but the forms crystallized only in the early Arabic writing in the later part of 1st millennium AD, or close to the year 1000.

It seems likely that the archaic Greeks took over the Proto-Canaanite Ѱ in the 11th century BC and used it for both *k* and *kh*. However, in order to distinguish between these two sounds, they adopted — in the 9th century — the Phoenician *kaf* 𐤊 which later developed into Ꝃ and K. (The form Ѱ was kept to designate *kh* in the western archaic local scripts.). This K was learned by the Romans and thus it became the eleventh letter of the Latin alphabet.

L

The earliest representation of the Latin L, Hebrew ל *(lamed)* and Arabic ل *(lam)* is a pictograph of an ox-goad (a spiked stick used for urging cattle) ϛ, ∽. These forms appear in the Proto-Canaanite script of about 1500 BC. The Phoenician script in the 11th century BC fixed the stance of the *lamed,* so that the curve was drawn at the base 𐤋, 𐤋. In the later Phoenician as well as in the Hebrew and Aramaic scripts, there was a tendency to sharpen the curve into an angle 𐤋. The diagonal upper stroke began at a higher point than the other letters of the alphabet, while the rightward base was drawn just beneath the ceiling line. In the 5th century BC, the Phoenicians added a leftward bar resembling a tail at the right extremity of the base of the *lamed* 𐤋. A similar development occurred in the fourth-century Aramaic script. The Aramaic *lamed* of this period consisted of a high vertical downstroke which curved to the right under the ceiling line L. The new form with the tail 𐡋 easily turned into a wavy line in the Aramaic cursive ⟆. (The Hebrew and the Samaritan *lamed* never developed such a tail.) The Jewish script preserved the tail of the Aramaic *lamed,* and it became a main part of the letter ל.

The Arabic script adopted the Nabataean cursive *lamed* (which is a descendent of the Aramaic wavy-line form) and straightened it. Thus the Arabic *lam* ل evolved.

Since the archaic Greek script was not a stabilized writing, the *lambda* was written either with the crook at the top ↿ or at the base ↾. In classical Greek writing, the first form prevailed and became Λ. But the Latin script adopted the latter shape and turned it into L.

M

The early ancestor of the Latin M, the Hebrew מ *(mem)* and Arabic م *(mim)* was drawn in the Proto-Sinaitic and early Proto-Canaanite inscriptions as a pictograph representing water. (The word in Hebrew for water is *mayim.)* The pictograph was drawn: 〰 or ⦚. In the later Proto-Canaanite script, the vertical zigzag prevailed, and was turned into in the tenth-century BC Phoenician script. Later the *mem* consisted of a zigzag-shaped head and a downstroke . The Hebrew forms were: → (cursive) and (formal). From this, the Samaritan developed. From the 8th and 7th centuries BC, the Phoenician *mem* was written which became in the Aramaic . In the late fifth-century BC and later Aramaic cursive, the downstrokes were bent leftward. Thus the medial and final variations evolved. These are the ancestors of the Jewish medial and final *mem* forms during the Herodian period, and of the modern Hebrew מ and ם.

The Nabataean *mem* was drawn without lifting the pen , and this led to the Arabic medial ـمـ and final م.

The development of the archaic Greek *mu* seems to be as follows: → → → . This means that the ancient Greeks took over the zigzag-shaped *mem* from the pictograph resembling water. It does not seem likely that the Greeks learned the form from the Phoenicians in the 8th century BC. At any rate, the *mu* developed eventually into M, which is the shape that still exists in both the classical Greek and Latin alphabets.

N

The earliest representation of the Latin N, Hebrew נ *(nun)*, and Arabic ن *(nun)* is a pictograph of a serpent . This developed in the later Proto-Canaanite and early Phoenician scripts into . Its variants in the various scripts were: Hebrew (Samaritan),

Phoenician 𐤍, and Aramaic 𐡍, 𐡍. During the late 5th century BC and after, the medial position in Aramaic writing bent the downstroke to the left 𐡍. Thus the Jewish medial נ and final ן *nun* forms developed.

The Nabataean cursive medial *nun* 𐢓 became more and more similar to medial *bet, yod,* and *taw*. In Arabic, the medial letters are written the same with only diacritical marks to tell them apart: *ba* (ﺑ), *ya* (ﻳ), *nun* (ﻧ) and *ta* (ﺗ).

The archaic Greek *nu* 𐤍 or 𐤍 resembles the late Proto-Canaanite and early Phoenician *nun*. As with the *lambda* (Λ) and *mu* (M), the length of the strokes of the *nu* became equal N. This form became stabilized both in the classical Greek and in the Latin alphabets.

O

Latin O, Hebrew ע *('ayin)* and Arabic ع *('ayn)* developed from the early Proto-Canaanite pictograph of an eye 👁. In Hebrew, in fact, the word for "eye" is the same as the name of the letter — *'ayin*. The pupil of the eye was preserved in some Proto-Canaanite inscriptions as late as the 12th century BC. However, it seems likely that it did not wholly disappear from the West Semitic writing until the early 11th century. The archaic Greek *omicron* was drawn as a circle. Sometimes it had a dot in its centre ⊙. It is difficult to believe that this dot remained from the needle of the cutting compass, as was generally believed. Rather, it seems to be representation of the eye pupil of the ancestral Proto-Canaanite *'ayin*. At any rate, the earlier pictorial form was replaced by a circle without a pupil or dot in its centre, and came to represent the Greek *omicron* and Latin O. Since the Greeks did not need this letter for the designation of the Semitic consonant, they used it as the vowel letter *o*. The Roman adopted the O with its value as a vowel.

In the Phoenician, Hebrew, and Samaritan scripts on the one hand, and in the South Arabic and Ethiopic on the other, the *'ayin* also has a circular shape, although there are certain variations.

In the Aramaic script as early as the 7th century BC, the top of the circle opens ∪ (compare with *bet, dalet,* and *resh*). It is written mainly with two bars (first to the left and then to the right) meeting at the base y. Since there is always a tendency when writing to draw the pen towards the next letter, the right bar becomes longer and longer y → y → y. In this way, the classical shape of the letter develops which is known in Jewish script to the present day: ע.

The Nabataean script also adopts this Aramaic letter. The Arabic ع (in final position ع) develops through the Nabataean cursive as follows: y → y → y → ع.

P

Latin P, Hebrew פ *(pe)* and Arabic ف *(fa)* stem from a common ancestor. In the Proto-Sinaitic inscriptions, this ancestral letter seems to be represented by the drawing of either a mouth (in Hebrew *peh*) or a corner (in Hebrew *pê'āh)*:), ㄴ. In the 11th and 10th centuries BC, in the late Proto-Canaanite and early Phoenician scripts, the letter was drawn as follows: 𐤐.

This form was accepted by the archaic Greeks. It had either a round head 𐤐, or a square one ⊓. In the classical Greek script, the *pi* with the square head prevailed and the short vertical bar became as long as the other vertical: Π. The Latin script adopted the round-headed form and closed the head ꟼ; or facing to the right: P.

Some varying West-Semitic versions of the *pe* are: Hebrew 𐤐 (Samaritan ࠐ), Phoenician 𐤐 and Aramaic 𐡐 → 𐡐 in medial and 𐡐 in final positions. The latter forms are the ancestors of the Jewish (modern Hebrew) פ and ף.

From the Nabataean 𐢛 (final) 𐢚 (medial), the Arabic ف *(fa)* developed. (The single diacritic mark distinguishes it from *qaf* ق, which developed from the Nabataean *qof.)*

Pe is used in Hebrew both for *p* and *f*. Since in the Arabic phonemic system there is no *p*, it served only for *f*. In Greek, its value is *p* (while *phi* Φ was added as a supplementary letter). In Latin, since the *vau* (the archaic Greek derivative of the *waw*) was used for *f*, P came to designate solely the consonant *p*.

Q

The earliest common ancestor of the Latin Q, Hebrew ק *(qof)* and Arabic ق *(qaf)* appears in Proto-Sinaitic inscriptions from about 1500 BC. Its form was 8. Later, closer to 1000 BC, it turned into 𐤒. In the archaic Greek writing the *qoppa* was written either Φ (as in the West Semitic script) or Ϙ. Classical Greek omitted the *qoppa*, but it survived as a numerical, designating the number 90. The Latin alphabet, however, preserved the letter and Q is used in several modern European languages.

In the West Semitic scripts, the *qof* developed in the 8th and 7th centuries BC as follows: the circle was opened 𐤒, it turned into two half-circles 𐤒 and then the left half-circle was drawn with the downstroke without lifting the pen 𐤒. The last form was preserved in the Hebrew script, while in other scripts the head of the *qof* formed an S in horizontal position. There were similar developments in Phoenician (𐤒), Samaritan (ࠒ), and Aramaic (𐡒). The later Aramaic and Jewish *qof* reduced the left curve of its head ק.

The Nabataean script went further and wrote the letter in this way: P. This developed ʃ → ʃ → 9 until it became similar to the *pe* (9). In the Arabic script, it was necessary to add diacritic marks in order to distinguish *waw* (و) between *fa* (ف) and *qaf* (ق).

R

The initial form of R, ר (Hebrew *resh*) and ر (Arabic *ra*) is a pictograph of a human head which appeared in early Proto-Canaanite and Proto-Sinaitic inscriptions, 𓁶. The Greek name *rho* seems to indicate that the Canaanite name of the letter was *rosh* (= "head"), while *resh*, the Aramaic word for "head", seems to be the Aramaic name of the letter.

In the late Proto-Canaanite script, the pictograph developed into a linear form 𐤓, which was preserved in the Greek *rho* P. Another archaic Greek variant R was the ancestor of the Latin R.

In the ancient Hebrew script, the closed top of the *resh* was preserved 𐤓 (Samaritan ࠓ). While the Phoenician cursive opened the circular head at its lower part in the 5th century, the Aramaic script opened the top of the letter by the late 8th century BC. (Compare with Aramaic *bet, dalet,* and *'ayin.)* Later, there was in the Aramaic script a tendency to write the letter without lifting the pen and then to curve its shoulder → and thus the Jewish *resh* ר developed.

Since *resh* and *dalet* resemble each other, they were often written in the same way in some scripts. In Syriac, only diacritic marks distinguish between them: ܕ = *dalet;* ܪ = *resh.* **In the Nabataean** cursive and hence in the Arabic script, the *resh* evolved into a single vertical stroke and has been assimilated with the *zayin.* It becomes necessary to put a diacritic point above the *za* (ز) in order to distinguish it from the *ra* (ر).

S

The earliest common ancestor of Latin S, Hebrew ש *(shin)* and Arabic س *(sin)* appears in about 1500 BC as a pictograph of a bow or . The late Proto-Canaanite *shin* was the model of the Greek *sigma.* In the archaic Greek script it had the following shapes , , S. While the first shape prevailed in classical Greek Σ, the Latin alphabet preserved the last form, S.

In the Phoenician, Aramaic and Hebrew scripts, this letter was written: 𐤔 .While the Hebrew script preserved this form (Samaritan

Ш), the Phoenician *shin* developed into Ѱ → Ш → Ш, and the Aramaic Ѱ → Ѱ → Ѱ. The last shape is the basic form for the Jewish (modern Hebrew) ש. From the Nabataean ש → ש evolved the Arabic س, which was used both for *sin* (س) and for *shin* (ش).

T

The basic pictographic shape of the Latin T, Hebrew ת *(taw)* and Arabic ت *(ta)* consisted of two strokes crossing each other: X or +. This is the simplest mark and hence its name is *taw,* which means sign or mark in Hebrew. In the Proto-Canaanite and in the early Phoenician scripts, until the 10th century BC, both the x-shaped and the cross-shaped *taw* were used. In the 9th century BC, however, the letter's stance was stabilized. The Hebrew script preserved the x-shaped X and did not alter its form, but in the Samaritan script it became ʌ/. The later Phoenician script adopted and developed the cross-shaped *taw:* † → ⺅ → ⺅; and in the Aramaic script it evolved as follows: † → ⺅ → ⺅. The last form was the model for the Jewish *taw* ת and Arabic *ta* ت.

The Arabic letter developed through the Nabataean ת → ת → ت → ت → ت. As the *ta* became similar to other Arabic letters, diacritic marks were added in order to distinguish among the medial forms of *ta* (ـتـ), *ba* (ـبـ), *ya* (ـيـ), and *nun* (ـنـ).

The archaic Greek *tau* is derived from the cross-shaped late Proto-Canaanite *taw* +. In the earliest Greek inscriptions, its shape is T, which was changed neither in the Greek nor in the Latin scripts.

Taw is the last letter of the West Semitic alphabet. The Greeks added five supplementary letters: *ypsilon* (Υ), *phi* (Φ), *chi* (Χ), *psi* (Ψ) and *omega* (Ω).

U

U has a relatively short history. This letter was introduced only in the early Middle Ages, as a variant of the V. In the original Latin alphabet, V designated both *v* and *u*. This invention was made in order to distinguish between the *v* as a consonant and the vowel *u*. (Compare with I and J.)

V

V is a derivative of the Greek *ypsilon,* the first supplementary letter. It comes after the letter *tau* in the Greek alphabet. (The *tau* developed from the *taw,* the last letter of the West Semitic alphabet.) The *ypsilon* was written in the archaic Greek local scripts as Y or Ỵ or V. The Latin script adopted the last shape. It designated both the vowel *u* (as in Greek) and the consonant *v*. Only in the early Middle Ages was U introduced to indicate the vowel *u,* as we have said before. Thus V remained the letter for the consonant *v*. (See below also, Y.)

W

W has an even shorter history than J and U. It was introduced only in the 11th century AD. In English it is a semi-vowel representing a sound between the consonant *v* and the vowel *u*. Its name is "double-u". In German, this letter stands for the consonant *v,* and the V is pronounced *f*. V in German is called *"fau"* and the W is called *"ve"*. However many European languages have no W at all in their alphabets.

X

X is the first original Latin supplementary letter. It was added to the alphabet in the second half of the 1st century AD and called *ultima nostrarum,* a Latin phrase meaning "the last of ours" and referring, of course, to the last of our letters. Its value is *ks*. Evidently it is a derivation of the Greek *ksi.*

The Greek *ksi* stands in the alphabet between N and O. Both its place in the alphabetical order and the shape of the letter correspond to the West Semitic *samekh*.

The *samekh* in the late Proto-Canaanite and the early Phoenician alphabets was drawn as follows: 𐤎. In the archaic Greek scripts, the form of the *ksi* was mainly 王, which turned into Ξ in classical Greek. But in the western local script, it was also written X. The Latin alphabet adopted this form later than the other letters. It enabled the Romans to copy Greek names such as Xenophon or Xanthippe, and to write in one letter the combination of *c* and *s* which sometimes occurred in the middle of Latin words.

In the Greek and Latin alphabets the consonant *s* is not expressed by the descendant of the *samekh,* but by that of the *shin*. Arabic *s* is also written with *sin* (س), which developed from the *shin*. The Nabataean *samekh* ([glyph]) fell into disuse.

The *samekh* of the 10th century BC 𐤎 developed in the Phoenician script into [glyph] and in the Hebrew script into [glyph]. The Aramaic *samekh* evolved as follows: 𐤎 → [glyph] → [glyph] → [glyph] → [glyph] → [glyph] → [glyph]. In the Jewish script of the Herodian period, it was written [glyph], which is basically the shape of the modern Hebrew *samekh* ס.

Y

Y is the second Latin supplementary letter, which was borrowed from Greek in order to represent the Greek *ypsilon* (Y). In English, it is used either for the consonant *y* or for the vowel. But in other European alphabets, the *y* is used either as a vowel or not at all.

Ypsilon is the first Greek supplementary letter. It is derived from the Phoenician *waw*. It seems likely that the Greeks adopted the West Semitic *waw* twice. At about 1100 BC, when the Greeks took over the Proto-Canaanite alphabet, they used the *waw* (in Greek *vau*), just as the Semites did for the consonant *v* (see above, F). Later, at about the 10th century BC, they adopted the Phoenician *waw* when they needed a letter for the vowel *u*. In classical Greek, *ypsilon* is pronounced as *ü*, or *i*, while *u* is written OY.

Z

Z is the last letter of the alphabet and is also a Latin supplementary letter. In the Latin language, there was no *z*. It was borrowed from the Greek alphabet in order to represent the Greek *zeta* in the Greek loan-words such as *zodiacus,* meaning zodiac.

In the Greek alphabet the *zeta* is the seventh letter. It corresponds to the West Semitic *zayin*. In the late 2nd millennium BC, the Proto-Canaanite *zayin* was written as follows: I. This was also the form of the archaic Greek *zeta* and only later it turned into Z.

The Phoenician *zayin* developed as follows: I → Z → ⋎. The Hebrew script preserved its original form I, while the Samaritan *zayin* developed into Ʒ. The Aramaic *zayin* evolved from the eighth-century Phoenician Z and in cursive scripts, it was written as a wavy line ˥. This later dropped its extremities and turned into a vertical stroke |. The vertical *zayin* was preserved in both the Nabataean and Jewish scripts. In Arabic, in order to distinguish *za* from *ra,* a diacritic point was added to the *za* ز. In the Jewish script, as the vertical stroke was interchangeable with the *waw,* a rightward hook was added to the letter top ↾. From this form the modern Hebrew *zayin* ז developed.

ILLUSTRATION SOURCES

Department of Antiquities and Museums, State of Israel P. 9, 11, 17, 24, 26, 27, 29, 30, 33, 40, 59. Staatsbibliothek Berlin P. 10. Cairo Museum P. 12. From Evans, The Palace of Minos P. 13. Dr. Georg Gerster, Zurich P. 16. M. Chuseville, Vanves P. 18. From F. Conti Rossini, Chrestomathia Arabica Meridionales Epigraphica P. 19. Giraudon P. 10, 21. Shikmona, Haifa P. 23. Louvre Museum, Paris P. 25. Prof. Y. Aharoni, Tel Aviv P. 28. Israel Academy of Sciences and Humanities P. 32. Brooklyn Museum P. 34. The British Museum P. 37, 38. The Turin Museum P. 39, 76. The Shrine of the Book, Israel Museum P. 44–46. Israel Museum P. 46. The Alphabet Museum, Tel-Aviv P. 50. Instituto Poligrafico Dello Stato, Rome. From "Epirafia Greca" by M. Guarducci P. 52-55, 60. Drawing by Ofra Kamar, Jerusalem P. 60 bottom. Photo D. Harris. Jerusalem P. 62. Bezalel Museum, Jerusalem P. 73. National Library, Paris, P. 74. Rheims Library P. 75. Section II letter drawings by B. Engelhard, Jerusalem.

INDEX